OUR CHURCH AND OUR CHILDREN

OUR CHURCH
AND
OUR CHILDREN

Sophie Koulomzin

ST. VLADIMIR'S SEMINARY PRESS
1975

Library of Congress Cataloging in Publication Data:
Koulomzin, Sophie.
  Our church and our children
  Bibliography: p. 157
    1. Christian education of children. 2. Orthodox
Eastern Church—Education. I. Title.
BV1475.2.K68   268   75-20215

ISBN 0-913836-25-7

© Copyright 1975

St. Vladimir's Seminary Press

PRINTED IN THE UNITED STATES OF AMERICA

BY

ATHENS PRINTING COMPANY

*TO ALL THE CHILDREN WHO
TAUGHT ME SO MUCH*

Contents

Author's Foreword

This book is my second attempt to present the sum of my thinking and experience in the field of Orthodox Christian education. The first one, *Lectures in Orthodox Religious Education* (Orthodox Theological Library I, St. Vladimir's Seminary Press, n.d.), was the substance of a course I was teaching at the Seminary then and is no longer available. Its contents would not be adequate today, for the educational movement within our Church in this country has progressed and developed, the situation in the parishes is not what it was twenty years ago, and my own thinking has developed further and has been shaped in the process of working and thinking together with others.

I realize that the present book is not an academic work. In the main it is an attempt to set down my philosophy of Orthodox Christian education—the philosophy of a laywoman, a teacher, a mother, and a grandmother. I am extremely conscious of its inadequacy, of the lack of research and preliminary studies in its preparation. The importance of the subject deserves a much more thorough book, but there is one reason and, I believe, a very valid one for its publication: there is no book in existence dealing with the mission of our Church today to the children living in our society here and now. A very modest and incomplete beginning is better than no beginning at all.

My sincere and warm thanks go to all my friends who gave me so generously of their time and advice, especially to Father Thomas Hopko for his thoughtful and constructive criticism, to Frieda Upson for her editing, and to Connie Tarasar for her work on the bibliography.

Introduction

There is no place for triumphalism in speaking of Christian church life today and of its educational task. In certain ways the period we are living through now has something in common with the earliest period of Christianity. Christian faith—in the sense of believing that Jesus Christ is God and Man, believing in the Holy Trinity and in the Church as the living Body of Christ—is held by a small minority, and this small minority is splintered and divided. Christian symbols, Christian traditions and feasts have lost to a considerable degree their inner vitality. They have either faded out of our life or have become commercialized or identified with culinary and ethnic customs and reduced to a rather general concept of good cheer. In large parts of the world it takes courage to admit that one is a Christian. Even when there is no official enmity to religious faith, our entire culture has become divorced from religion. In all the impressions to which an average modern child is exposed at home, at school, through mass media, through library books, magazines and advertisement, one would be hard put to find any Christian content or any Christian understanding of life values. To a considerable extent this is true even in church-going families. In this sense a child grows up today in a situation rather similar to that of a child growing up in the days of the Roman Empire.

The big difference is that today there is no clear distinction between a Christian and a non-Christian world-view. In the Roman Empire, general school education was completely secular. The prevailing concepts of marriage, of family relations, of human personality were very different from those of the Christian community. A Christian child grew up in his home imbued with the consciousness that to be a Christian meant to be different from the surrounding society, to reject its values. "Adjusting to the environment" or "fitting in" was inconceivable. Today the dividing lines are blurred. What does it mean to be a Christian? Who claims to be a Christian today? Theological distinctions are eroded. To be "dogmatic," to be "doctrinal," is perceived as a negative quality. Equally eroded today is the identification of Christianity with a certain social respectability, so prevalent a generation or two ago. And it is difficult to blame the younger generation for rejecting the hypocrisy of this kind of Christianity, even though there was much more than mere hypocrisy to it.

Many people who call themselves Christian claim that Christianity means to them the Sermon on the Mount, a way of living in a relationship of love and respect for other people, of peace and good will, coupled with a vague feeling that there does exist a Divine Power in the world. Up to a point, one cannot question the sincerity and the validity of such an attitude. Yet we cannot claim that moral values and ethics are the distinctive and exclusive domain of Christianity. Not only do all religions have a code of ethics, but even such movements as Communism or Nazism have a very demanding code of moral standards: of discipline, self-sacrifice, comradeship, obedience to authority. A textbook on ethics for teacher training institutes published in the Soviet Union has quite a nineteenth-century flavor when it deals with courtesy, obedience, honesty, cooperativeness, etc. Thus if we say that Christian morality is the essence of Christianity, we have to make clear and understand just what Christian morality is and how it differs from moral behavior in general. Here we face a paradox: Christianity is unthinkable without its moral implications, its moral law; and yet moral law can exist completely divorced from the Christian concept of life and can even be violently inimical to Christian faith.

Thus we face today, in educating our children, a situation similar to the one that had to be faced by the early

Church. And yet there is a great difference. We cannot
simply adopt the piety of the medieval man. Certain spiritual
values and postulates are part of our thinking today. Belief
in man's freedom under God, belief in his creative task in
the world, respect for human individuality, and tolerance
were always an intrinsic part of Christian thought at the
level of great saints and theologians, but they were not reflected in the life of society, in the pattern of home life or
in pedagogical theories. Inquisitions, religious persecutions
and wars, harsh discipline in the home and at school, and
intolerance were not motivated by "badness." They were
part of a generally accepted and recognized method of "sav-
ing souls."

For many centuries educational philosophy, whether secular or Christian, took for granted that each child's soul is
a "tabula rasa." Protect the child from exposure to bad influences, punish misdemeanors, recompense good actions,
and the end product will be a good person.

Though one of the main points of Christian spiritual
guidance—as seen, for example, in the *Philokalia*—is that
each soul is absolutely unique and that the spiritual father's
task is precisely to discern what is right for the spiritual
growth of each particular person, this approach was not reflected in the general practice of the religious education of
children. Individual spiritual fathers and saints had a remarkable measure of this personal insight, but the effort
to understand the individual child, to recognize his inborn
talents and traits, to encourage his creativity and self-
expression, to understand the "reason why" of his behavior,
was not part of the religious educational program of the
Church as a whole.

The principle of man's freedom under God has gained
great importance in recent times. It is *the* concept that
distinguishes our Christian world-view from modern anti-
Christian dictatorial philosophies. The act of Christian faith
is a free act. Faith does not impose itself with the obvious-
ness of something you cannot deny. It is a "conviction of
things unseen" (Hebrews 11:1). There can be no faith without freedom, you can truly believe only if you are free to

doubt. All this was implicit in Christian theology of all ages, but it is only fairly recently that it has become such a part of man's Christian conscience.

This has a deep influence on our entire approach to Christian education. It means that we can expose a person to what we believe, to the reality of faith in our life, but we cannot *make* anyone believe, and, by extension, we cannot *make* anyone believe correctly. The ultimate act of faith has to be a person's own free act. This insight lies behind the generally accepted principle of religious toleration, and this is why we cannot accept the principle of authoritarianism as a method of religious education. It does not mean that we do not accept authority. Obviously a great part of our faith is based on trust in the authority of someone—of saints, of the Church, of the Holy Scriptures. But this very trust is an act of free choice and cannot be imposed. Authoritarianism as a method of religious education simply does not work any more. We cannot tell our children and young people: "You must believe thus and so because I say so, or because it says so in the catechism, or because it is in the Bible..." We can and must say: "I believe...," "the Church teaches...," "It is written in the Gospels..." But our educational work should be based on the presupposition that any child or young person can attain faith only in an authentic free act of his own. This is why we need to understand our children, their emotional and intellectual development, their motivation. The child's way of thinking and his imagination must become part of Christian education in a way not considered in the past.

The Orthodox Church today faces a challenge. It needs to discover an approach to religious education that is rooted in the total church tradition. This tradition includes knowledge of God, the life of grace within the Church, relationships with others. At the same time Christian education has as its object the education of a person. Whether it deals with an infant, a young child, an adolescent, or an adult, it must deal in a personal way with the individual at whatever level he exists: speaking his language, understanding and sharing his needs and concerns, loving him as he is. Religious experience is valid at whatever level it takes place, at any stage of intellectual maturity; and the process of Christian education must be a process of growth that is each person's own experience, a gradual change involving his total person. The task and the challenge are tremendous and can only be met if we live fully the life of the Church. The task of Christian education must be an expression of the charisma, the grace, of the Church as a whole.

Against this background of the challenge of our times we can better understand the more specific problems confronting the Orthodox Church in America today. Several important facts influence the situation: Orthodoxy in America today is still in the process of emerging from being an "immigrants' church," of being the ethnic home away from the old country. There are quite a few parishes that are still precisely that. With each succeeding generation, however, this ethnic character of church life is more and more eroded. Ethnic traditions become more and more superficial, less and less connected with truly religious values, and yet they remain important for a number of people. Answers to questionnaires sent out to parents in 100 parishes in 1972 indicated that 70% of the parents found "traditions inherited from their own parents" the most helpful influence in bringing up their children as Orthodox Christians. Eighty-nine per cent mentioned "attending church services"; 56% mentioned sermons; 19% mentioned religious books. On the other hand, dynamic younger church people are becoming strongly convinced that the very nature of the Church is violated by identifying it with an ethnic ghetto. They feel that Orthodoxy cannot and must not remain "Russian," or "Greek," or "Serbian," or "Ukrainian," that the Church is above all national distinctions.

This trend, however, leaves unresolved a very important problem. Orthodoxy and church life are not abstract concepts. Neither are they completely expressed in doctrinal teachings and theological formulations. The living cells of the church body are precisely those "home churches" so often mentioned in the Epistles. The very nature of a "home church" involves the incarnation of religious values and beliefs in simple daily practices, behavior patterns, celebrations, meals and other usages deeply rooted in tradition. A family is more that just father, mother and children. A family is heir to the moral and spiritual patterns and values cultivated in the homes of the parents' parents, grandparents and great-grandparents. We are constantly reminded of this in the Biblical stories of the Old Testament patriarchs. It is very difficult to create a rich Christian home life in a sterile laboratory environment, free of all traditions. From this point of view American Orthodoxy is growing through a difficult and demanding period, a process of gradually creating its own traditional patterns. I believe that it can only be helpful to this new tradition if threads of the old country religious-cultural heritage are woven into the new fabric.

Another aspect of Orthodox life in America today is the strong emphasis on the importance of Christian education given in parish church schools, often called Sunday Schools. In new parishes educational buildings are as carefully planned as the church itself. Some new school buildings are amazingly well equipped, almost luxuriously, especially since they are used only one hour a week. The lay church school teachers (a fairly new tradition in Orthodox church life) have been in a very real sense the "growing edge" of the Church, demonstrating a remarkable degree of responsibility and devotion. In the process of giving themselves to the Church, they have often been the ones who have achieved the greatest growth in stature as members of the Orthodox Church.

This concern for education was probably caused by the realization that the simple piety of early immigrants did not "carry over" too well into the life of next generation. This second generation became very often the "lost one" for Orthodoxy in America. It seemed then that the only way to preserve the Orthodox faith was to give our children a better formal education in it. Many hundreds of Sunday Schools were created in Orthodox parishes of all national backgrounds, with all teaching done in the English language. "If only we could put all of the essential Orthodox teachings into one small booklet," I heard a priest say some twenty years ago, "we could make sure that every child in our Sunday School really learns to know it and our problem would be solved."

This educational optimism proved to be unjustified. Moreover, the Sunday School movement proved to carry certain dangers within it.

The worst was the practice of holding Sunday School on Sunday mornings during Divine Liturgy. In the absence of a vigorous, authentically Orthodox tradition of Christian education, this practice was taken over from Protestant groups. It was gladly accepted by children and parents, because children were bored by long church services in languages that they did not understand and during which they had no opportunity for participation. Yet what happened was that children were never introduced to the fullness of corporate liturgical experience, with entire families attending together. The Sunday School replaced the Divine Liturgy, the classroom lesson replaced the sacrament. Students graduating from Sunday School had not acquired the habit of going to church on Sundays. The life of worship, which is the essence of Orthodoxy, was thus undermined.

Another danger lay in the tendency of identifying religious education with classroom instruction. The underlying idea seemed to be: let the children learn to know the contents of the textbooks and this will make them good Orthodox Christians. Rather quickly the unsatisfactory character of existing textbooks was recognized by teachers and priests. Formal catechisms, memorization of prayers, vocabulary and texts were felt to be exceedingly boring, and they were supplemented by sweetly sentimental "children's versions" of Bible stories and by little songs and games from old-fashioned Protestant collections, very often quite unsound doctrinally.

The Orthodox Christian Education Commission, in whose work representatives of practically all Orthodox jurisdictions in America took part, came into existence in 1957. It pioneered in producing manuals that tried to bring the fullness of Orthodox faith and life closer to the children's experience and to appeal to the children's creativity. Efforts to revise and improve textbooks and teaching aids are still going on; and the work of the Commission, its workshops, and its teacher training seminars have done much to encourage the educational work of Orthodox churches in America. Yet there is a growing realization that classroom instruction and textbooks are effective only when they are part of the total church life—the life of liturgical worship, of Christian home life, and of Christian community life. The child learns to be a Christian only within a living Christian home, and within a living and worshiping Christian community.

Thus the educational work of the Church has to be three-dimensional: building up a full liturgical life in the parish, reaching the parents and the home, and instructing the children. Any one of these aspects cannot exist and grow by itself. This total task is what the Orthodox Church in America faces today.

response, a real understanding of what religion means, a capacity to feel and think religiously.

To acquire the sense of the reality of God is the goal of our whole life. Obviously no textbook, no lesson, no activity *per se* can give it. But I do believe that this basic purpose should always be kept in mind by the teacher and should serve as a criterion for all our teaching methods, our lessons and activities.

We are a Body

Within our Orthodox experience of Christian life man is not *alone* under God. *We,* all together, are with God. We are gathered under God. We are one: one Body. The small family unit, the larger fellowship of friends, the nation, the church are all aspects of this oneness of many. At each level it is a potentially religious experience, and if it is not part of our Christian education, there is something wrong with our approach. The experience of group play in the church kindergarten, the relevance of class instruction to the older child's relationships with friends and neighbors, the realization of responsibilities on a social and national plane, the communion of church life, are all part of the gathering of the Church.

This experience of being part of a body belongs to the essence of religious growth. An infant deprived of the experience of belonging to a close organic family unit is tremendously handicapped. His spiritual and even his physical growth suffers. When a three- or four-year-old comes to nursery school, the most vivid impression is not the story told, but the round game, the song, the action, the very fact of being part of a group. Routine actions, like hanging up one's coat, or moving one's little chair quietly, so hard to teach at home, become a fascinating way of acting "like the others," of being a member of a group.

The best size for a class is one in which children can be seated as a group working together, with the teacher a member of the group; the best teaching techniques are those that provide projects on which children work as a group, even though there must be opportunity for individual creativity. The best school is the one that is part of the community or the parish, when parents and teachers have a close relationship. Liturgical worship in church is truly liturgical when it is an experience of "gathering together" as the whole Church, of *doing something together.* For mature Christians this means worshiping together, praying together. They can do it in their minds and hearts, with a minimum of physical action. For children this participation in worship must express itself to a much greater degree in physical action, involving their physical senses. There are many opportunities for this in Orthodox services, but we must learn to discover and to use them. Through such "active" participation children can gain a better understanding of becoming part of the Body which is the Church.

As years go by, much of the information we teach our children may be forgotten, but if they have shared this experience of being part of the Church, of belonging to a Body, of establishing personal relations within the group, and if this group is identified with the Church, then we have laid a solid foundation for Orthodox Christian education.

Religious education means growth

Religious education must involve growth. Growth means change. One grows from something one is into something one was not, and yet one continues to be the same person. Growth is a process that takes place within the individual: he grows in understanding, in strength, in intelligence, in feeling. When there is no growth there is stagnation. The whole art of education can be defined as "stimulating growth." This sounds trite, yet it is one of the most demanding and critical criteria to be applied to the educative process. To what extent does our lesson stimulate growth? To what extent does it *stretch* our students' capacities? To what extent does our teaching provoke an autonomous process of growth in the students' capacities?

We find an excellent illustration of this approach to teaching in the Gospels. The teaching technique most widely used by Jesus is the use of parables, i.e., a "language of art" in which a familiar image of everyday life is introduced to make the listeners discover and perceive a deeper truth. Teaching in parables demands an effort of imagination and understanding on the part of the listener. He has to discover for himself the meaning of the image. This is a creative act. Once the idea is perceived, it can be developed and consequences can be drawn. The first step, however, is to perceive the image, to identify oneself with the person in the story, so that the experience becomes one's own. This is a far more "growth-producing" way of teaching than is presentation of a syllogism, a logical structure that is irrefutable.

Another aspect of the method of teaching of Jesus Christ is that He approaches each person at that person's own particular level of development. Jesus does not reveal Himself fully from the start, and the Gospels refer several times to the fact that "they understood Him not." Nor does He reveal Himself to every one of His listeners in the same way. The growth of understanding on the part of the disciples is a very gradual, individual process.

Within a family, Christian education does not mean simply making the child conform to family standards in a passive, static way. Christian education involves the recognition of constant change in the child: change in his perception of love, of unity, of obedience, of joy and sorrow. The "reason why" a child obeys changes and grows from the purely physical submission of the young child to a recognition of the moral authority of the parents, and the "reason why" a child rebels changes accordingly.

One of the hardest tasks for parents is to give up seeing their child as a baby, to recognize changes in their child's tastes. Occasions of great joy, like birthday parties, or picnics, or camping trips may suddenly lose their attractiveness for a youngster. Hardest of all is to give up the aura of omnipotence or omniscience with which a young child endows his parents. But unless the child grows and changes, unless his own perception of his role within the family and of his relations with others changes, his development is arrested.

In a classroom situation, growth can be encouraged only when the teacher involves the student's interest, doubt, acceptance, challenge, search, problem-solving in the contents of the lesson. Ideally the teaching process should consist of confronting the student with a problem—a problem well at his level and that he can recognize as such—and then of furnishing him the information he needs to solve the problem. Merely conveying a package of information is not sufficient. All the techniques to "make lessons interesting," all the newest gimmicks and audiovisual aids are really worthless unless they involve an authentically creative effort on the part of the child and thus encourage his growth. This is a demanding criterion to apply to all activities in the classroom. Poster-making, puppet shows, or even role-playing and discussions can be as uncreative, as enforced, as any old-fashioned recitation period. We do not encourage growth by speaking about it, or explaining it, but only when our method of teaching involves creative effort, trial and error, research and problem-solving.

Holy Mystery, the "Fear of God"

Our teaching of faith has to be a reasonable one, a "reasonable service" (Rom. 12:1), and yet our faith goes beyond the rigid framework of reason. The sense of the holy mystery of God, the standing in awe of God, or fear of God, is an essential part of our faith. Christian faith involves the recognition of the mystery of God, of a whole world, a whole life beyond human understanding. It sees our life here and now within the perspective of values and realities beyond our experience. How can this be reflected in the process of religious education, a process which is primarily a process of reasoning? How can we, in teaching children to "understand," teach them at the same time to

stand in awe before something that is beyond their understanding and ours?

To make this task even more difficult, we have to recognize that children are naturally great realists, full of
cheerful curiosity. Any attempt to convey a sense of awe,
of holy mystery, through verbal formulations simply does
not reach them and may seem a rather hypocritical pious
formula. On the other hand we have to keep in mind that
the word "fear" in the expression "fear of God" means
something very different from many other kinds of fears.
Children are open to many fears—like fear of the dark, fear
of loud noises, fear of spiders, etc.—and to identify the
"fear of God," the sense of awe, with a fear of frightful
things, in other words to frighten children, is certainly not
helpful in learning to know God.

It would be a mistake to believe that reasoning and
knowledge are inconsistent with awe in facing the "Un-
understandable." As a matter of fact we cannot recognize
that something is "un-understandable" unless we have an
experience of understanding. Perhaps this is why it is difficult for children to experience a sense of awe. They don't
have sufficient knowledge and understanding to sense that
there are things beyond human knowledge and understanding. I would say that it is much easier for an Einstein to
experience a sense of mystery and awe, than it is for an
eight-year-old, who is sure that his third-grade textbook gives
all the answers.

Our task in developing the children's sense of awe is
to help them recognize God's action within the realm of
their experience of life, of their knowledge of natural events
and of their reasoning capacity. At their own rate and in
their own way, with God's help, they will acquire a sense
of the holy, a sense of awe before the mystery of God.

The following passage from a manual written for young
teenagers explains rather well this kind of approach:

> Science offers man much truth. The truth of
> facts—hard concrete and inescapable facts. But is
> there not more to life than the truth of facts? For
> example, how do we factually define the difference

between the moment *before* a man dies and the moment *after* he dies? If a man is on the operating table and something goes drastically wrong, there is a moment when the doctors can save him, and there is a moment later when it is too late. His life has slipped away. In concrete terms this moment cannot be biologically pin-pointed. Some cells will be dead long before, and others will be alive long after. But an indescribable difference of quality takes place: one moment the person is alive, and the next moment he is dead.

In the face of this mystery science is helpless. The truth it offers, its facts, its figures can make distinctions of quality, distance, time, etc. but the distinction of meaning occurs only in *"life thinking."*

Science thinking seeks answers to problems; *life thinking* seeks answers to mysteries. There is an important difference involved. A problem has a definite answer, a solution. However difficult problems in science may be, however distant is the time when their solution may be found, they always have answers. But a mystery has no pat answer. How can one say, what is life, what is sorrow, what is joy? All one can do is gain a deeper insight into the mystery of these things. Losing someone you love, nursing him or her through a sickness, and seeing your loved one die can make you gain a deep insight into the meaning of suffering. These insights are what we call truths in *life thinking*. The deeper the insight, the profounder is the discovered truth. As one begins to comprehend sorrow, to know joy, to understand good and to recognize evil, one begins to see Truth. One begins to approach the core of the mystery.*

---

*G. Koulomzin, *Faith and Science* (published by the Orthodox Christian Education Commission, 1969), chapter 3.

A good Christian teacher should prepare himself to make use of all the material presented in the public school curriculum, to point out the kind of knowledge that is given there, what this knowledge answers and what it cannot answer, and to relate it to our religious concept of life.

Wholeness

This aspect of "wholeness" in religious education should not be isolated from the other points I have made. What it means is that Christian faith can never hold an isolated position in our life—whether in the individual life of a person or in a person's relationship to the world he lives in. You cannot be "partly Christian," or a "part-time Christian," nor can you be Christian in only certain parts of your world.

All of man's nature, all of his gifts, all of his feelings, all of his relationships and his actions, all of his interests are part of his religious life. Our Christian faith does not deal with only one of the sections of man's nature. In his encounters with the people who came to Him, Jesus constantly emphasized the need for His followers to commit themselves *wholly*. The rich young man, almost perfect in most respects, could not commit himself fully and turned away. The apostle Peter, though he failed several times, gave himself wholly and became the greatest among the apostles.

If we accept this, it has to be reflected in the way we teach our Christian faith to our children. The teacher in the classroom is concerned not only with Johnny's knowledge of the words of the Creed (though it *is* important to know and understand the Creed) but with Johnny as a whole person. And Johnny is very quick to sense this, even though it is not put into words. If the teacher is able to establish a relationship of friendship with Johnny as a person—and such a friendship does not exclude being exacting—it will probably affect Johnny more deeply than a class project or the information given. Seeing Johnny as a whole person means simply being interested in him as an individual, try-

ing to understand why he behaves, feels and acts the way
he does, trying to become familiar with his home and his
background, trying to judge his work not only in comparison
to the work of the others, but for what of himself he puts
into it.

Christian "wholeness" is shown by the teacher in his
own attitude to what takes place in class. He cannot be
narrow-minded; he has to show interest in a lot of matters
that seem important and interesting to his students. His
influence will be greater if his students find him unexpectedly knowledgeable about matters that have nothing to
do with church school but are important to them.

In our pluralistic, secularized society the concept of the
Church is often reduced to that of an isolated, self-enclosed
body that has nothing to do with the concerns of the world.
Of course, in a sense Christians "are not of the world,"
but only in the sense that they do not accept the secular
hierarchy of values. The Christian Church should be an
icon of love and concern for the whole world, and thus it
cannot stand in isolation, unconcerned. It should be concerned and compassionate toward all the needs and suffer-
ings of all people. Can we teach this to our children, under
the usual conditions of parish life? Can we teach without
hypocrisy something that is not really practiced in life?

I believe that in a very modest way we can do this. We
can grasp every practical opportunity to involve our church
schools and our children in projects and programs that en-
large their experience in relationships. Visits to churches of
different ethnic traditions in connection with class work,
participation in assisting others' needs, interest in the
Church's missionary work—all of this is possible and helpful. As the children grow older we can present to them
a deeper understanding of the Church's concern for all
the world.

To sum up this chapter, I believe that an Orthodox
Christian approach to religious education must include these
five objectives:

— To help children gain a sense of the reality of God
in our life.

— To make them realize that none of us stands alone under God, that we all are part of a Body, the Church.
— To cultivate authentic individual growth of mind and
spirit.
— To bring children, as they grow older, to recognize
with awe the holy mystery of God, beyond the limits
of human rationality.
— To help them realize that Christian faith is not a
water-tight compartment and involves the whole person and all of life.

I realize that these objectives are a rather imponderable
and in a sense indirect complement to the immediate aim
of any school education: the conveying of information, the
elucidation of reality, the guidance to truth, the attaining
of insight and understanding. We are immediately concerned that our students know the facts, and it is in connection with knowing the facts and seeing the point and
understanding the situation that people believe and do whatever they believe and do. This direct and obvious purpose
of church school instruction will be dealt with in later chapters. But I am deeply convinced that unless the imponderable
objectives described in this chapter motivate and inspire our
teaching, it will lose a lot of its vitality and meaningfulness.

CHAPTER II

Our Children

Before we approach the subject of the content and methods of Christian education we must focus our attention on the children whom we wish to educate. What are the stages that they go through, what are their needs and readiness for learning, what are their interests and capacities?

Infancy: age 0 to 3

During this first period of childhood, called by Piaget the *sensory motor stage,* a baby grows in less than three years from a small, helpless being that cannot control its sight or its movements and is completely inarticulate, into a small human person that walks, runs and speaks; expresses his desires, his likes and dislikes; recognizes and loves certain persons; dislikes or is afraid of others; can be amused, curious, happy, sad, angry, frustrated; has associated a number of things and people with pleasurable or irritating or frightening feelings; knows love, pity, jealousy. By the end of this period he has fairly well discovered the world of the home and its immediate vicinity; he has accumulated an immense number of impressions. He has a vivid fantasy, though no formal intellection. His intelligence expresses itself in actions. Towards the end of the period he is ready for ideas based on the discoveries made by his senses: bigness and smallness, colors and shapes, etc.

More than any other tradition, the Orthodox Church emphasizes the religious importance of infancy. During the very first weeks of his life the infant receives three sacraments—Baptism, Chrismation and Holy Communion—and is the object of special church services: the naming of the child and the churching. The Church makes the infant a bearer of grace and protects him from the power of evil long before he shows any hint of awakening intelligence and understanding. It seems as though the Church recognizes thereby the whole realm of development of the subconscious—the "self" deeper than the level of thought and will. The ascetic, spiritual tradition of our Church understands that the "self" which we know, accept and even "create" is just the "tip of the iceberg." There is the much greater part under the surface, which is not known but is tremendously active in determining our lives. And this very important and critical depth is formed almost exclusively in infancy. In a certain sense all of adult life is reaction to a development received in infancy.

On the conscious level we can roughly summarize the mental and physical processes that go on before a child is three years old as follows:

1. Discovery of his physical self, the development of physical senses, sight, smell, touch, movement, taste, hearing.

2. Discovery of freedom and restriction, of acceptable and unacceptable behavior, feeding habits, freedom and restriction of movement, toilet training.

3. Discovery of security and love. For example: the sensation of cold, wetness and discomfort is replaced, when the mother approaches, by warmth and comfort. The sensation of hunger is relieved daily by the same person. Sensations of pain are relieved and comforted. A little later, the fear of being lost, even within one's own home or yard, is dissolved when the same person appears and the whole world becomes safe and stable.

4. Discovery of negative feelings: rage, fear, jealousy.

5. Discovery of the discrepancy between his own will

and the imposed will of another, usually adult person. A complicated emotional pattern arises in a child when the source of all his well-being suddenly turns against him and becomes an enemy imposing unpleasurable experiences: surprise, aggressiveness, trying out his own power, occasional submission or resentment.

6. Accumulation of factual experiences and information without being ready to intellectualize about them. Impressions and images are preserved, sounds and smells are remembered, but the infant is unable to grasp a logical sequence of cause and effect that adults take for granted.

7. Towards the end of infancy, between the ages of two and three, the child usually acquires the ability to express his wishes in words, to communicate with the surrounding world through talking, however primitive.

The bringing up of the infant takes place in the home. The parents, or those who take their place, are the only educators the infant knows. Throughout infancy we can only speak of education as a total process of growth within the relationship of the close family unit. We cannot separate this process into physical and moral education, we cannot speak of "instructing" the infant, even though he learns so much during these first three years.

In a very real sense we can speak of the "priesthood of parents." Their task is almost sacramental, for they bring God into the life of their infants and offer their infants' life to God. There is a holy "wholeness" about the task: the way a mother changes a baby's diaper, the way she feeds him, the way she cuddles him, is as meaningful for the religious growth of the child as the way she prays over him or the way she brings him to church. Whatever a mother does for the baby is religiously meaningful if through this action and relationship she expresses love and care and conveys a sense of security and happiness. The quality of that love will be affected by the kind of relationship the mother has with God. A mother's love can be possessive, jealous, insecure, or full of fear and anxiety; in some cases a mother can be so unhappy, or selfish, or confused that she simply does not love her child. In such a case the infant is truly religiously deprived. But the joyous, responsible, self-sacrificing steady love that many mothers give their infants is religious in its very nature, whatever the mother's beliefs may be. An unafraid, joyous baby, eagerly discovering himself and the world he lives in, is a religiously wholesome baby.

The mother's love can link the baby to the religious experience of adults, to their life of prayer and to their participation in the liturgical life of the Church. The baby's perception of this religious and sacramental life may seem to be purely sensual, but it is nonetheless fully authentic.

One of the very striking passages in the Gospel is the validity Jesus Christ ascribes to the pre-intellectual experience of religious faith. When His disciples, in an effort to maintain an adult level of teaching, tried to prevent mothers from bringing their children to Jesus, He "became indignant." He said that to such belongs the Kingdom of God, and that whoever does not receive the Kingdom of God as a little child shall not enter it (Mark 10:13-16). He illustrated God's relationship with little children: He took the children in His arms and blessed them, laying His hands on them. He gave His love, not through teaching, not even through a story, but through bodily contact. He made them feel His closeness through their physical senses and, speaking to adults, He stressed that the children's perception of His love, the way in which they received the grace of His blessing, was valid and religiously meaningful: "Whosoever does not receive the Kingdom of God as a child shall not enter it."

Our church life offers many opportunities for such a perception of religious values through the senses. Let the baby handle his baptismal cross; let him see, touch and kiss the icon over his cradle; let him feel the smell of incense and the bright colors in the church building; let him receive Holy Communion with his lips and feel its taste; let him feel the sprinkling of holy water on his face, hear the singing, make the sign of the cross, even though it is only a kind of finger play for him. In our Church all these physical objects, sensations and experiences are not merely religious baby-talk to be discarded later. Each of the things I mentioned remains a perfectly valid, meaningful action, gesture or experience throughout an Orthodox Christian's life. The baby enters into them, begins to participate in them through his own, perfectly authentic infant experience.

The capacity of the very young child to accumulate images, impressions, and factual information should be nourished religiously. Just as the parents expect their children to learn the words of the adult language they hear around them, just as they help them to learn about their environment—that fire burns, water is wet and snow is cold—just so should they let them imbibe religious impressions and ideas. Let the children see their parents pray; let the parents give religious interpretations of what the children see; let the children attend church services where they see, hear, taste, touch and smell objects of great religious meaning. We must remember, however, that it will be through the parents' sincerity and authenticity of devotion that all this will acquire a truly religious meaning, will serve as an introduction to religious experience.

A young mother of two babies told me once: "I know why Tania (two months old) is fond of attending church. At home I am always so busy, there is so much to be done; but in church, for a full hour and a half, she can stay in my arms, at peace, without my jumping up to do something else." I truly believe that such a peaceful experience of love and security in church is very close to an experience of worship.

Towards the end of infancy little children grow open to the festive mood of all kinds of celebrations—Christmas, Easter, birthdays and namesdays.

Though we cannot speak of the infants' "moral consciousness," they do go through many experiences that prepare them for later moral concepts. The discovery of freedom and restriction, of security and love, the discrepancy between one's own will and the imposed will of another, the unhappiness of fear and jealousy, the pleasure of approval—much of this experience acquired in infancy is basic to our religious development. The infant will make these discoveries whether his home is Christian or not, but in a Christian family these experiences are illumined by the spiritual life of the parents.

Over and above all we have mentioned in speaking of religious growth in infancy, there remains the holy and mysterious action of the holy grace of God that touches it. No one can measure or evaluate precisely the effect of the sacraments which our Church gives to young babies. In faith and awe we can only make sure that these channels of the gifts of the Holy Spirit are kept open in the life of our children.

Pre-school children: age 3 to 6

In the Piaget table of stages of development this corresponds to the *preoperational stage*. Brother John F. Emling, in his excellent booklet summing up Dr. Piaget's chart of development stages, writes:

This *pre-operational stage* is marked by many characteristics, one of which is egocentrism. In the early years of his development the child is not able to take the viewpoint of another person. Moreover he has a tendency to focus his attention on only the more striking aspects of persons and things. Human characteristics and powers are given to inanimate objects as a result of the child's inability to separate and categorize reality ... Also the child considers himself the cause of every event. Yet, even if the child renounces considering his actions as the cause of every event, he nevertheless is unable to represent to himself the action of bodies except by schemata drawn from his own activity.

In this stage the child has a reason for everything and every question has an answer. Every answer makes sense to the child regardless of the logic used.*

This is the youngest age group with which we usually come in contact in most of our church schools. By now the children have acquired the art of more or less fluent speech and the art of understanding speech. Not only parents, but friends, teachers, and outsiders can communicate with them through talking, and the powerful tool of story-telling and verbal communication can be used. Stories, however, have to be very carefully chosen and presented.

Pre-schoolers at the younger level can listen to short stories lasting not more than five minutes, and at the older level not more than ten minutes. A story has to make a constant appeal to their physical senses, through actions that involve the children in repeating the sounds, imitating the movements, showing how big and how small are the things mentioned, looking at large and clear pictures, touching objects brought to illustrate the story. The story plot should be very clear and simple, one event at a time, with no reference to concepts of chronological time and/or distances. "A long time ago," "yesterday," or at the oldest level "when I was little" are all the concepts they have of past time. Places in the immediate neighborhood, "not far from here" and "far, far away" are all the concepts they have of distance. Abstract concepts like "truth," "nation," "goodness," "justice," "power," "faith," and even "love" are quite foreign to their mentality, though they can understand that a person is "nice," "kind," or "nasty" and "unkind." A teacher should never make an appeal to emotions with which little children cannot identify.

The young child's moral development is very primitive, though he may have assimilated some of the verbal moralizations that he receives so plentifully at home or elsewhere. "Bad boy," "good boy," "naughty," "good"—how often does a child hear these words! Yet he is quite unable to

---

* "In the Beginning Was the Response," *Religious Education*, Vol 69 No. 1 (Jan. 1974).

recognize independently whether an action is good or bad, why curiosity and desire to know is commended when it is applied to some things and why it is reprehensible at other times. Just as he was accumulating facts about his physical environment and capacities at an earlier age, so is he now accumulating experiences of approval and disapproval that will gradually form his ideas of right and wrong. A five-year-old will recognize that "God wants us to be good" and that "we must not be bad," but what is "good" and what is "bad" is still very hazy and is simply identified with approval or disapproval. Ideally, approval or disapproval in the Christian home and a Christian environment will begin to build up the child's framework of ethics.

Thus the basic ideas of sin, repentance, redemption, death, resurrection, life-after-death are completely beyond our pre-schooler, though the feeling of "being naughty" or of "being forgiven" is within his experience. He may also know of someone who died, or of a baby born, but his ideas will be very primitive and tied up with the externals.

Children of this age group need constant physical activity and cannot stay quiet long. Their need is for large gestures, simple movements, not complicated by too many rules. Creative work in class should be planned for this.

The child is ready to make things. He has the control of his larger muscles, and though fine work is beyond his skill, he enjoys using colors, blocks, clay, sand. The creative instinct is unhampered by self-criticism. Any work has to be short, with immediate and visible results. Very often the meaning that the child puts into a picture is not obvious to others, and it is helpful to have him explain what the picture means. There is no need for fancy equipment, but whatever room of the house is used, there must be easily accessible work space with plenty of elbow room, even if this means newspapers all over the floor.

The young pre-schooler is extremely individualistic. It is very rare that children of this age spontaneously play *together,* maintaining two roles that complement each other. Joint play activity with another child is more like two separate activities running parallel. This is to be remembered when activities in the classroom are planned.

The ability to coordinate one's work and play with that of other children is perhaps one of the major skills achieved at the pre-school stage. Taking turns, following instructions and simple rules, becoming conscious of the other children, feeling part of a group with certain very simple responsibilities—all these are very important abilities developed at this stage. "Round games" and simple dramatic and singing games are excellent in nursery school and kindergarten. Competitive games, games with more or less involved rules, games requiring skills, and team games are not suitable.

Desire for approval and recognition—strong at every age—plays its part too. The ability to perform correctly in public, to imitate adult gestures and behavior is very satisfying, and training in church behavior is willingly assimilated, unless it is "pushed" too hard on the child and causes an obstinate refusal to conform.

There is very little capacity to distinguish between the real and the fantastic. How often will a little child begin to tell about an actual happening and, as the story progresses, introduce into it completely fantastic details. If church school teachers could hear the versions told at home of the stories they have so carefully taught, they would certainly be surprised.

Today the pre-schooler's world is not completely limited to the home, but parents are still omnipotent beings. There is no danger from which the child does not feel he can be protected by his parents; there is no tragedy beyond "Mummy, fix it!" Under ideal circumstances such an experience of a "loving and just omnipotence" is very helpful in developing the child's idea of God.

Five-year-old children are quite ready to hear a very simply told Bible story of creation. The children can take active part in the story: ask them to close their eyes in order to "feel" the darkness there was before God made light, and to open their eyes to "feel" the light. They should be given opportunity to touch leaves and flowers and seeds; they can act out how different animals move, how birds fly.

Stories illustrating how God cares for us can be told. The story of Noah's ark, emphasizing how God saved Noah and his family and families of animals and how the dove flew out and brought back a green twig when the flood was over, can be told, dramatized and played at. Stories like the one of baby Moses in the bulrushes and Jesus calming the tempest are also suitable. Equally good to tell are simple stories of miracles, emphasizing not the miraculous aspect (which children will not understand) but showing that Jesus cared for people and helped them. The story of Adam and Eve in the garden, of Adam giving names to animals, of how Adam and Eve lost the garden, and of God's promise to them can be told simply and factually without expecting the children to understand the concepts of "fall," "sin," or "salvation history." The story of Jesus Christ and the little children and the nativity story are always well liked. The same stories can be told over and over again, with the children actively participating in them, just as favorite games are played over and over again.

A five-year-old child, growing up in an Orthodox Christian home and drawn in some way into the educational life of the parish, will have accumulated quite a number of religious concepts and experiences. He will have some idea of God who made everything, who is kind and very powerful. To a certain extent the child transfers to God the qualities of authority, love and omnipotence of his parents. The nature and character of the parents will affect deeply the child's religious consciousness. He will have some idea of Jesus Christ as a person from the stories he has been told and from the pictures he has been shown, but he will have no idea as to whether "God" and Jesus Christ are two different persons, nor will he feel the need to clarify this concept. An Orthodox child will learn to make the sign of the cross and to say the words "In the name of the Father and of the Son and of the Holy Spirit," but usually this is not connected with stories told, and it seems too early to attempt to explain the doctrine of the Holy Trinity.

A child's concept of the Church is identified with the church building. The more familiar he is with its details, the more at home he will feel in it. He will feel satisfaction in knowing how to "perform" correctly—make the sign of the cross, kiss the icons, approach Holy Communion, receive a blessing and join in some of the singing. Of course, this knowledge is mechanical and external, but it gives the child a sense of belonging, of being at home in the church, and this feeling goes deep.

A major element in the young child's experience of church life is frequent communion. This is the point where the Holy Mystery that lies at the heart of Christian faith penetrates into the life of the child. The reality and the validity of the sacrament cannot be identified with the child's rational understanding of it. From the reverent attitude of the parents and of the congregation the child may realize that there is something special about the act. Explanation cannot go much further than saying that Holy Communion is the holy food God gives us. One can say that this is the food Jesus gave to His disciples when He had supper with them for the last time, and that every time we eat this holy food, it is like Jesus Himself giving it to us.

Attempts to explain to very young children the words "Take, eat, this is my Body which is broken for you..." and "Drink ye all of this: for this is my Blood..." can be disastrous. I know a case when awkward, though very sincere attempts by a church school teacher to explain the meaning of Holy Communion to young children led to a painful scene in which all the children, obviously frightened, refused to approach Holy Communion on Sunday. The best approach is to tell children towards the end of the three to five age group the story of the Lord's Supper, telling them that this was the way Holy Communion was given for the first time, that Jesus Christ Himself gave it to His disciples, using the very same words we hear in church now and that He told us to do this in His memory. The children's attention can be focused on the icon of the Last Supper which is often seen above the Royal Doors.

A five-year-old living in a Christian home should have acquired quite a lot of experience of celebrations and traditions through which he learns much of the Christian view of life. Christmas, Easter, weddings, baptisms, funerals, the blessing of homes are colorful events that deeply affect the child's consciousness.

A child of five is certainly no *tabula rasa* as far as religious education is concerned. Under favorable conditions he has accumulated a lot of religious impressions that can grow and develop later. Even if he has received no formal religious training, but has grown up in an atmosphere of emotional security and love, within a framework of discipline involving the whole family, he is in a state of readiness for conscious religious growth. If he has been deprived of such a background, he has suffered a real deprivation. His "spiritual unconscious," which is the ground and foundation for future voluntary and conscious thought and action, has been formed.

Middle childhood: age 6 to 10

The children in this age group have thoroughly emerged from the world of the immediate family environment. They attend school, they have friends and enemies of their own whom their parents do not know. They have to make judgments and establish relationships on their own. They have to adjust to the rules and relationships of a larger world—the school, the neighborhood, the street block, the summer camp. They are sent on errands, or they purchase things at the store for themselves. They learn to know laws—not only the rules established by their parents, but school rules, or those represented by the policeman on the street, or the rules established by other kids. Everything that they took for granted until now is gradually being tested and subjected to comparison. As their recognition of laws and rules grows, so also grows the temptation to break them—to steal things, to use bad language, to envy others for the things they have.

The child has to establish a new pattern of relationships with peers. Many children have a hard time harmonizing these relationships. They can no longer be satisfied with remaining individuals isolated in their work and in their play, yet they have not learned how to play and work together. The quarrelsomeness which they show at this age is a kind of embryonic expression of group spirit, for they are trying to establish new patterns and are rubbing off sharp edges. They can *consciously* suffer from a sense of betrayal or rejection in their relations with other children. A child's best friend suddenly switches to a new friend, and even if this is temporary, the suffering it causes is sharp and real. The teacher has a tremendous prestige, somewhat displacing that of the parent. New enmities and affections create a larger and richer emotional environment.

An important mental development takes place during this period. A sense of cause and effect is developed, an ability to organize and classify that which is concrete and real for him. He is interested in simple planning and in the carrying out of a plan. We can see this reflected in their play. This will not be simply the repetition of a pleasurable action—dragging toys, making simple block structures, throwing and catching a ball; it can be quite involved and complicated, such as having a club, forming simple team games, playing at war, playing hospital, or pretending to be on a radio or TV program, or being a secretary, or having adventures in which they act out their roles.

This change in mentality will affect their interest in stories. They will show interest in cause and effect, and, in listening to Bible stories, will show interest in God's plan for the world. I knew a seven-year-old who, upon listening to the story of the Fall, asked with exasperation: "But why, why could not God make Adam and Eve so that they would not *want* to disobey?" The boy was quite ready for a rudimentary explanation of the doctrine of free will. Explanations of doctrinal truths, such as the Holy Trinity (the well-known comparison to the shape, the light and the warmth of the sun, for instance), seem to be very satisfying and answer their liking for simple logical structures.

We should use this capacity for simple planning in carrying out class projects. Our difficulty, of course, is that church school meets once a week, and it takes more than rudimentary planning to remember projects from Sunday to Sunday. Still, in comparison with younger groups, when we have to treat every weekly lesson as if it were a separate unit and when the children's memory of the preceeding lesson is quite indistinct, we can do some planning and carry over unfinished work, with the teacher helping to revive the children's memory and interest at the beginning of the period.

There is now a far clearer consciousness of "justice" than there has been before. The instinct of ownership was already present at a much earlier age, but now there is a fairly clear understanding of what is "mine" and "not mine" (with a very great respect for my own rights and very little respect for the rights of others). Yet these rights are recognized and understood and quite often are violated with a full consciousness of a law being broken. The idea of "fairness" has a most Old Testamental flavor, with an intense insistence on justice and little readiness for mercy. Childish lies are not merely fantasy but are occasionally purposeful and conscious—an effort to avoid the unpleasant consequences of one's action.

Along with the sense of "law" and conscious "law-breaking," there is a growth, a development of finer feelings: compassion, desire to protect someone weaker than oneself, acceptance of certain moral standards and willingness to accept a certain amount of hardship for loyalty to them. I remember a little seven-year-old girl in a group of children attending one of the long Holy Week church services in a Russian church without pews. "Wouldn't you like to sit down?" I whispered to her. Looking at me very solemnly she whispered back: "We shouldn't always do what we'd *like* to do, should we?" They can also feel very sincerely sorry for their misdeeds.

In his book, *Readiness for Religion,* Ronald Goldman summarizes as follows the basic religious needs of middle childhood:*

Security—since the adults have lost some of the

Readiness for Religion (New York, 1970, The Seabury Press) pp. 105-118.

stature they had in earlier childhood, there is
need for some sense of "cosmic security," "an
ultimate faith in the kindliness of the universe."

Community—a feeling of the school community as
one where they are secure.

Standards—increasing awareness of the need to
observe standards acceptable to adults.

Meaning—on a concrete and limited level, the middle child needs to relate his many diverse activities to each other. Strangely, our religious
education, instead of providing a unifying idea
for all of life, is separate and divisive, set in
the context of an unknown culture of long ago.
The separateness is emphasized by an association
with just one day a week—Sunday.

Fantasy and imagination—because the child cannot
cope intellectually with the task of unifying and
relating all experiences to what he knows and
understands, he will resort to understanding
through imagination and fantasy. Where they
cannot think their way into an experience, they
can at least feel their way into it.

How then can we present God to children of this age
group in a way that relates to their experience of life? In
other words, are they ready in any way for Christian doctrine?
Can they participate meaningfully in liturgical worship?
What kind of message can they receive from the Bible?
What spiritual and moral values can be meaningful for
them?

Within the last decade Christian educators have been
greatly influenced by the writings of Ronald Goldman, who
did considerable research concerning religious instruction
given in English day schools. In England Bible study is part
of the general school program, is given by lay teachers, and
holds the same place as any other academic subject. Goldman
showed by numerous tests that children gained practically
no understanding of the meaning of the Bible narratives

as they are taught in school. He suggests that instead of
Bible teaching, children be taught by means of themes based
upon their real life experiences, such as: homes, friends,
people who help us, pets, shepherds and sheep, hands, feet,
clothes, breakfast time, seeds, birthdays and parties, etc.
He suggests that any of these themes may have a "religious"
and Biblical illustration, they may begin with a religious
emphasis or end with religion as a focal point.

Much can be said for this approach and none of it can
be simply rejected. Yet I feel quite strongly that this way
of teaching does not adequately serve the object of Christian religious instruction. A lesson or discussion *about* homes,
about friends, *about* pets is not the same thing as the
experience of having a home, having a friend, having a pet.
It can easily become an intellectualized or sentimentalized
abstraction and remain foreign to the child's own experience.
Our purpose is to awaken in the child a consciousness of the
presence of God, of His action in our life, of our relationship with God. Bible stories are a reflection of precisely
this reality, the reality of an encounter with God. The
stories are inspired, vivid, simple, having a real artistry of
language. I think we would be justified in interpreting the
traditional expression "God-inspired" as "a work of genius."
A well-told Bible story can become an experience introduced into the life of the child. It can produce an impression. Of course, the teacher has the task of interpreting this
new idea or impression in terms of the child's experience of
life.

What are the doctrinal ideas, "ideas about God in relationship to man," that we can convey to children of the
seven to ten age group?

They are ready to receive the idea of God as creator of
the universe. This idea can become religiously meaningful
only if they have experienced some wonder at the created
world. Unfortunately church school textbooks do not go
further than rather sentimental phrases about the beautiful
stars, clouds and mountains. The children should be exposed
to the experience of wondering at natural events. For example, the Biblical words "And God said, let the earth bring

forth grass, the herb yielding seed, and the fruit tree yielding fruit" can be made meaningful to children if we have
them watch the process. Simple experiments can be carried
out in class, or a film shown on the growth of plants. Many
other aspects of creation can be illustrated in similar ways.
Children can help make up posters on the use of water, on
fire, on the atmosphere, etc. It will be very helpful for the
teacher to become acquainted with science textbooks used in
the corresponding grade in public school and thus illustrate
in imaginative ways the story of creation. It will help to
overcome the divorce in the child's mind between church
school teaching and what he learns in public school, a
divorce that prepares the way for keeping religion in an
isolated compartment, a "Sunday knowledge" that has nothing to do with "week-day knowledge."

Another idea about God that children are ready to assimilate is that God cares for us, that he protects us. Here
again we have to face children's experience of life, their
nascent ability to submit things to the test of comparison.
All kinds of accidents and tragic events are seen on TV
and are part of the child's daily fare. Bible stories like that
of the three youths in the furnace cannot be used as a proof
that we need not be afraid of getting burned. The real point
of the story is the answer given by the three youths to the
king: "If it be so, our God whom we serve is able to deliver
us from the burning fiery furnace; and He will deliver us
out of your hand, O king. But if not, be it known to you,
O king, that we will not serve your gods" (Daniel 3:17-18).

There are many Bible stories that tell about God's care
in moments of danger, of God letting people suffer for some
time, but always remembering them and turning their suffering to their good. Children can recognize that difficulties may be necessary in order to guide a person. The story
of Joseph, the story of Balaam and his ass, of the prophet
Jonah and many others are good for this purpose.

Though it is too early to discuss with children the problem of suffering, and especially the suffering of the innocent, it is sometimes unavoidable. We can establish in
their minds the image of Jesus Christ as the one who was

innocent and accepted suffering, but His suffering and death were not the end, because He rose from the dead. If the children have really assimilated with their minds and their hearts' compassion the story of the Passion and the Resurrection, we have provided them with a basis for a Christian approach to the problem of suffering. They will have to deal intellectually with it at a later age.

Until children have accumulated a store of well-remembered and well-liked Bible stories reflecting God's love, God's care and His protection, it is worse than useless to teach them the bare statement "God loves us," "God is Love," "We must love God."

Speaking of teaching doctrine, we come to the concept of the Holy Trinity. Children have learned the use of the words "In the name of the Father and of the Son and of the Holy Spirit" at an even earlier age, since these are used so constantly in all forms of our worship. We should now add basic images that will nurture a better understanding in our seven- to ten-year-olds of these words. Of course a precise doctrinal understanding of the Holy Trinity is beyond the intellectual needs and capacities of children in the seven to ten age group, but we can supply images and narratives that will prepare them for a more mature understanding later. These narratives should be simple, but they have to be doctrinally correct, not something to be unlearned later.

Here are a few examples of Biblical stories used for this purpose:

1. Middle children are ready for the question "Who made the world?" and are also ready for the answer "God made the world." The teacher can then add a further question: "But who made God?" which will very probably puzzle the pupils. The teacher can then say that nobody made God, that God *was always.* She can then read aloud the words with which the Bible begins: "In the beginning God made the heavens and the earth. The earth had no form and the Spirit of God hovered above the waters. And God said: 'Let there be light.' And there was light" (Gen. 1:1-3).

The words tell us something about *who* is God. God

the Father made the world by His Word. Jesus Christ, Son of God, is also called "Word of God" (Logos) and the Holy Spirit of God fluttered above the empty waters. So you see that in the very first sentence of the Bible we learn that God—Father, Son, and Holy Spirit—made the world.

2. In telling older and more thoughtful children that God made man, we can also use the words of the Bible: "Let us," says God, the Holy Trinity, "make man in our image and our likeness, and let him rule over all living creatures" (Gen. 1:25). How, then, is man "like God"? How is he made in the image of God? Well, he must take care of the world (a little like God the Father). He is a reasonable person, and in the language of the Bible "word" (Logos) also means "reason." He is also a "spiritual" person: he can pray and love and think and feel more than just his body feels. So we can say that there is a little of the Holy Trinity in every human person.

3. Orthodox children often see in church the famous icon of the Holy Trinity depicting the visit of the three angels to Abraham. The story of the visit can be told without difficulty and the icon shown to illustrate it. Children's attention can be drawn to how the three persons are drawn into one circular movement, form one circle. In the case of the famous Russian icon, the teacher may add that the icon was painted by the artist Andrei Rublev, who lived at a time when his country was divided by many bitter quarrels, and that, as he painted, he prayed that the oneness of the Holy Trinity depicted in the icon would help people to become one in the love for their country.

4. The story of Epiphany or Theophany can be told, stressing how people on that day saw Jesus, the Son of God, heard God the Father's voice and saw how the Holy Spirit of God fluttered above the head of Jesus.

An abstract definition of the Holy Trinity seems to be beyond the intellectual needs of the children, but it may happen that a child will come up with a question: "How come, one God and three Persons? Has he got three faces?" No abstract explication is completely adequate, but one of

the more acceptable ones is that of a family. How many
are there in your home? Father, mother, one or two brothers
or sisters? You see, there are several of you, but you are
all together *one* family. In a family we quarrel sometimes,
we don't always love each other, but the Holy Trinity is
really all love, so that the three Persons are really one God.

Personally, I have always found it helpful at this point
to remind the children of the element of holy mystery when
we speak about God. A good story to illustrate this is that
of St. Augustine who, walking on a beach and meditating on
the Holy Trinity, saw a little child making a hole in the
sand and trying to fill it with water. In reply to his question,
the child said that he wanted to pour all of the ocean into
the little hole. This made St. Augustine realize that it is
just as impossible for the human mind fully to understand
the nature of God.

A very difficult aspect of religious education is that of
teaching children to pray. At an earlier age, the very action
of standing or kneeling, of making the sign of the cross,
of repeating certain words is sufficient to establish for the
child the fact of prayer. Now their daily private prayer
hovers somewhere between a dutiful repetition of prayers
learned by heart (which is not completely meaningless, for
it is a recognition of prayer as an attitude and a duty) and
an occasional spontaneous prayer of asking: "Please, God,
make the weather good tomorrow!" "Let me get a bicycle
for my birthday!" "Let her get well!" Both these aspects of
prayer are valid and legitimate, but something more is
needed. This "something more" cannot be imposed by anyone, it can only be born within the child. The educator's
task is to make sure that the habit of prayer remains as a
kind of discipline and that the procedure of prayer does
not become mechanistic to the point of obstructing the possibility of authentic prayer. It is helpful to suggest that
children pray for matters of real concern—for someone they
know who is sick or in trouble, to thank God for some
special gift they have received, to ask God's help in something they find difficult to do. Group prayer at the beginning of church school is often quite a problem. It is very

difficult to establish a prayerful attitude at this time of gathering, with some arriving late, others eager to talk to each other, teachers trying to establish some kind of order, etc. I have found it helpful to say a word or two to focus the children's attention and establish quiet before the prayer is sung or read. For example, before a group began to sing "O Heavenly King," I reminded them that this is a prayer to the Holy Spirit, the Holy Spirit "Giver of life," who fills with life all things. "Let us see whether we can sing the prayer in a way that will show there is life in it." At other times one can draw their attention to some key word or to the event with which the prayer is connected.

Children within this age group, as far as I can observe, find it more difficult to attend church services. They are less of a disturbance for the adults and are more used to services, but very often they find them extremely boring. When the service is held in English and the children have been taught at home or in church school to understand what it means, the difficulty is reduced, but still the obligation to remain completely quiet and inactive, with nothing exciting to watch for a fairly long stretch of time, is often a burden. Very small children are diverted by watching the lights, the bright colors, sensing the unfamiliar smell, hearing the singing, but for the older children all this has lost its novelty. The requirements for good behavior are more strict and the passivity of participation is irksome.

Some liturgical instruction at this point can be very helpful. Interest in what they see in church will be stimulated by a study of the church building, with explanation of the purpose, the meaning and the use of all the objects. Learning about the saints and events shown on the icons gives them something to look at and think about. Understanding the order of the Liturgy, the sequence of the major moments, will help them to follow the service. Teaching all this should involve a lot of the children's own creative activity—simple models, diagrams, pictures, calendars, etc.

More effective than any of this instruction is to find opportunities for children to participate *actively* in the service. A junior choir may be allowed to sing some of the responses, as many altar boys as possible should be enrolled, girls can be involved in the decoration of the church, in putting up and taking down candles, distributing leaflets, etc. Whenever a procession is held, a special effort should be made to involve the children. Different opportunities can be found according to the local customs and traditions, but it is important to keep in mind the desirability of finding opportunities for children's active participation.

Both teachers and parents can direct the children's attention to observing things during the service in church. How often does the priest use the Gospel book? How and when does he use the chalice? How many processions do we have during the Divine Liturgy? How many saints can you recognize on the icons? Such and many similar questions can be distributed by the teacher to the children before they attend the Divine Liturgy and results can be checked on the next Sunday.

Yet, when all is said and done, we need not feel upset that for many children going to church remains an effort. Effort is an important part of religious life, and to recognize that we do certain things, not only when we feel like it, but because it is our duty, is a wholesome thing.

With children in the seven to ten age group we can go a little further in explaining the meaning of Holy Communion. The main emphasis remains on the Last Supper and on what Jesus Christ did and said. We can now add the idea of *gifts*. Receiving and giving gifts means a great deal to children of this age. They count on gifts, they expect gifts and they think about gifts. They are also very eager to give gifts—preparing gifts on Mother's Day, making endless lists of people to whom they propose to give gifts at Christmas—all this is very important to them. We can tell them Old Testament narratives about gifts and sacrifices brought to God, and these stories will serve as a background for a beginning understanding of the gift of His life brought to us by Jesus Christ. The idea of sacrifice should not be merely a matter of a one-time explanation, but it can be illustrated and presented through many stories. Holy Communion is Jesus Christ's gift to us, the holy food, the holy meal which He shares with us so that we can live with Him. We accept this gift, and we try to bring Him our small gifts, by trying to live the way He wants us to live. These ideas have to be presented through stories and examples, with only very brief and simple explanations; but impressing the child's mind with these images serves as a kind of preparation for growth and understanding.

A major event in the liturgical experience of children during their middle childhood is being admitted to the sacrament of Penance or Confession. The three sacraments they have been receiving until now were given without demanding understanding on their part. But the sacrament of Penance involves a real, personal feeling and understanding. This church practice is, of course, not accidental. It presupposes that a child of seven or eight has reached "the age of reason," i. e., that he can make a conscious choice between what is good and bad, that he can sin and repent. This involves a major challenge for Christian education: the need to develop a child's ability to recognize sin in terms of his own life experience.

Generally speaking, children within the seven to ten age group accept the principle of obedience. "To be good" means to obey one's parents, one's teachers. To disobey means "to be bad." They also recognize and accept the principle of "fair and unfair," usually in the form of protesting against unfairness to them: "The teacher is unfair!" "You cheated!" Boys will tend to admire bravery and courage as a virtue even when used unwisely, like climbing to some dangerous place. Girls will be more open in expressing feelings of tenderness, compassion and affection. Jealousy, feelings of inferiority, of being rejected, are quite frequent, but almost subconscious, unreasoned. The "sins" generally recognized as such by children are those of breaking some rule or doing something forbidden. Carelessness resulting in disaster, like breaking something or causing an accident, is readily recognized as sin. Children accept unquestioningly the family standards and use them as a yard stick to decide what is right and what is wrong.

This concept of morality as obedience to rules of behavior is strongly supported by the society in which the child lives, whether the society is nominally Christian, neutral, or even hostile to Christianity. In any society the morality of obeying rules is indispensable as a kind of "natural morality."

The Christian concept of morality that we have to teach to our children goes deeper. We have to help them realize the meaning of sin as a *break in relations,* rather than the breaking of a rule. In practice this means that throughout childhood we have to develop the child's appreciation of personal relationships, beginning with the relationships with people of the immediate environment and carrying on into relationships with God. The difficulty is that verbal definitions do not convey these meanings to children. The child has to experience what it means to "be trusted" and "to trust," to understand and recognize what other people feel, to be compassionate and friendly, to forgive and be forgiven, to receive help and to give help. We can do this through stories chosen so that children can identify themselves with the events told in the story. Having the children spontaneously "act out" and dramatize the story helps them to gain a better insight into its meaning. One of the most satisfactory experiences of this kind that I have had, was acting out, with a small group of children seven and eight years old, the sin of Adam and Eve and then the sin and repentance of the Prodigal Son. The spontaneously improvised dialogue between the "serpent" and "Eve" showed real insight:

"Did He forbid you to eat fruit?"

"No, He did not—just from this special tree."

"Why?" (Very innocently)

"Well, He said we'd die."

"He did, did He?" (In a very sly manner. Then in a conspirational whisper) "Well, what He said is untrue! If you eat this apple you will become like God Himself!"

"Oh, you don't mean to say so! It can't be true! Do you really mean we'd be like God?" (Energetically) "No, I won't do it!" (Coyly, after a pause) "Is the apple really as good as it looks?"

There, dramatically expressed, with hesitations and pauses, were all the steps of temptation clearly shown by two little girls seven and eight years old. And they had no difficulty in finding for themselves the difference between Adam's self-justifying attitude ("She gave it to me!") and the Prodigal Son's repentance ("I am unworthy!").

The key theme of moral education through middle childhood is the development of the child's realization and appreciation of the relations that link him to other people and to God. The concept of repentance is part of this: a broken relationship can be mended, by being sorry, by forgiving and being forgiven, by making up. The key theme of repentance is the desire to mend a break in relations, and God is always, in every case, willing to make up.

The experience of being admitted to the sacrament of Confession is very critical in another sense too. Until the age of seven, children receive Holy Communion frequently, often every Sunday. Upon reaching this "magic number" they sometimes suddenly come to a stop and are relegated to receiving Communion once or twice a year. Preparing the child for his first confession is a very important part of pastoral care. The priest can then decide whether the child is ready for confession. Some children may be ready earlier, others later. And, most importantly, the first confession must not be a "cut-off" point for regular communion.

Only a priest who actually hears children's confessions can have a full insight into the nature of confession. Father Thomas Hopko makes the following comments:

> The main problem with this age-group in relation to confession is the *dual* character of a person's approach to God:
>
> 1. God gives laws which we must obey, we must do good.
>
> 2. God forgives us and loves us and never puts us off, no matter what bad things we do, if we are sorry and try to do good. But still we must do good.
>
> I have seen at this age already the tendencies

either to feel "It's OK, everyone is bad, God forgives" or extreme frustration and despair. Until
now a child always felt he or she was "doing
good." Now there is an awareness that one "does
bad" *even when one tries to be good,* that it does
not work. Dealing with one's badness is critical in
human life and it is first learned at this age. It is
very difficult to make the child realize that both
indifference ("I can't help it!") and an attitude
of despair, frustration, anxiety, are wrong. The
child must learn to face badness in himself, and
to realize that he will fail and still must keep trying. With God's and others' help he can succeed,
though he will never be sinless.

Late childhood: age 10 to 13

The older children grow and the more complex they
become, the less open they are to the comparative stranger,
to the teacher in a church school. By now they have been
moulded into a certain shape, into certain patterns of behavior that were superimposed on their natural character.
They have been exposed for years to the influence of their
family background, their parents, brothers and sisters and
relatives. The cultural and ethical standards of the family
have influenced their attitudes, made them different from
each other. Whatever their special situation within the family did to affect their personality—jealousy, rejection, pos-
sessiveness, competitiveness, etc.—has left deep traces. They
are less spontaneous and more self-conscious than at an
earlier age.

For eleven- or twelve-year-olds Tommy or Suzy, their
parents are no longer the omnipotent figures of earlier childhood. They have had time to evaluate them and compare
them with other people in their friends' homes and at school.
Pre-adolescent rebellion begins to work up. Curiously enough,
they are almost fanatically partisan of the way "things are
done" in their home and believe it to be "the" way, but at

the same time they are critical of the way their own parents treat them and are easily irritated by their brothers and sisters.

Church school teachers have another difficulty in trying to relate to the students' homes. As church school instruction progresses, it often happens that the religious ideas conveyed there are not in agreement with the concepts of the parents. We are living at a time when Orthodox parents, as a rule, have received in their childhood very little instruction and rather poor instruction regarding their Church. Thus the teacher has to show great understanding and tact when dealing in class with a child's statement "Yes, but Daddy says that..." or "Mother says that the Church teaches..." The teacher must always try to see the element of truth in whatever beliefs are held at home: "Yes, this is very interesting. I think the reason for this is that..." He can then add and expand the ideas he wants to convey.

Relations between boys and girls are very self-conscious. They are very definitely two different groups—usually critical of each other and slightly inimical toward each other. Occasionally mutual attraction may be felt by a boy and a girl, and it immediately becomes a subject for teasing, very often in poor taste. For years already they have been influenced by the over-emphasis on sex in everything they see around them—TV programs, commercials, advertising. The boys' ideas of masculinity and especially the girls' ideas of femininity are deeply affected by these images. Little girls will assume sophisticated postures and gestures, attempt to use make-up indiscriminately. Boys will collect "dirty" pictures and "dirty" books, use "dirty" language. Most of this is still a kind of play-acting, a thing of imagination. By extension they will say that a picture of Adam and Eve in Eden is "too sexy." An excellent picture of a naked child in a Roman Catholic booklet on the five senses was said to be "dirty."

It seems to me that the sex education programs included in the health courses in public schools are not very helpful. Obviously some knowledge of the physical aspect of sex is just as necessary as information about other physical functions of the body, but there are at least two main differences. Sex education given to older children is involved with deeper emotions, with many conscious and half-conscious feelings stronger, for instance, than dental hygiene. And rightly so, for sex is a very important part of the growth and development of the person and cannot be separated from the basic concept of the meaning of human life. Man-woman relationships are part of God's plan and can be seen in their right perspective only in the light of a religious concept of life and of human personality. Treated exclusively from a physical point of view, without reflecting any of its "meaning," sex becomes rather cheap. On the other hand the physical aspect of sex belongs to an area of intimacy. Violating this tradition of intimacy seems to me very questionable. Treating a vital and intimate personal relationship as if it were an ordinary school subject does not teach children to understand it better. I heard a thirteen-year-old girl complain that she went to the trouble of memorizing fifteen methods of contraception for her examination and then found that only five of them worked and only these had to be learned. It seems to me that the task of Christian education is to help ten- to thirteen-year-olds develop a concept of what a human being is and to understand better God's plan for man-woman relationships.

What level of intellectual ability have these older children reached? How well can they think, how much intellectual luggage have they accumulated that will allow them to judge, to compare, to evaluate?

Ronald Goldman writes of late childhood and preadolescence:

> The search for meaning is now at the start of a new intensive phase, for the onset of clearer thought creates problems in the child's religious ideas. Childish concepts are clung to, but the doubts and confusions are already appearing. At previous stages the child happily kept together unrelated and often contradictory ideas, but now he is becoming aware of the need to relate and reconcile these apparent contradictions. We require

an intensive effort in teaching religion at this
stage to help him grow into a "one-world" view
of life, rather than a dualistic system which sep-
arates religion from the rest of life.*

The faith we bring them has to be a "reasonable faith."
They can understand a lot; they want to understand; a
kind primitive scepticism is not foreign to them. They are
quite good at understanding and following a logical structure of thought, even abstract thought, if the sequence of
ideas is clear, simple and *brief*. Interest and attention lag
if the explanation or sermon is long. They will willingly
accept rather simplistic formulations if they sound logical
to them. An intelligent eleven-year-old boy told me: "Oh
yes, I understand the meaning of salvation. Before Jesus
Christ came everyone went to hell. After He came and died
and rose from the dead, everyone can go to Heaven." The
definition was clear, simple, and it satisfied him. The teacher
has to have a real theological maturity to be able to put
down things clearly, simply, briefly and yet in a way that
will allow the germ of a doctrinal idea (an idea about God
and God's relationship with men) to grow and develop to
a greater fulness.

Another type of thinking that one frequently meets at
this age is a conscious separation of knowledge into two
different parts—one that I learn at school, read about in
books, or hear about on TV, and the other that is taught in
church and in church school. A twelve-year-old girl, brought
up in a conservative Orthodox environment, told me once
rather desperately, when the theory of evolution was mentioned in a conversation: "No, I've decided to believe in
Adam and Eve!" Obviously she had compared, judged,
hesitated and finally decided she would hold on to this in
the teeth of anything that might be said in favor of science.
I tried to explain to her why I thought that there was no
real conflict between the faith of the Bible and science,
and she seemed surprised, relieved, and even excited.

The children's knowledge of the Bible, especially of the

Readiness for Religion, p. 138.

New Testament, is very uneven. There are a few stories that they have heard over and over again, and this gives them a false sense of "knowing" the Bible. "Oh no, not about Him again!" was a typical reaction when the study of the life of Jesus Christ was introduced in the sixth grade. On the other hand their ignorance of the Scriptures is really abysmal, both of facts and of meaning. Not even the Sermon on the Mount has reached their attention in full, and they have no idea of the meaning of the Old Testament, except for a few stories about Adam and Eve, Noah, Abraham, Joseph and Moses. The Old Testament as a foreshadowing of the New Testament is very little known or understood. Yet they try to figure out and find explanations satisfactory to themselves. In a group of twelve-year-old campers, talking among themselves, the children were shocked by the statement made by one of them that the Last Supper was a Jewish feast and that Jesus was a Jew. They were quite proud of the answer they made up: "Yes, perhaps Jesus was born a Jew, but He was *baptized!*"

I purposely quote all these authentic samples of the children's reasoning because it shows the level of thinking they have reached and the level at which we have to teach them. They want reasoning and logic, but their own reasoning and logic is very primitive. They will ask questions the teacher will find difficult to answer precisely because they want very simple and clear-cut answers. Their backgrounds vary greatly and the difference in degrees of maturity is perhaps greater now than at an earlier or later stage. And constantly bursting out is their very special sense of humor, quite crude sometimes. The church school teacher often has a difficult time knowing when to share the joke and see what is funny and when to stop a kind of clowning that verges on the irreverent.

By the end of late childhood a person has accumulated the basic knowledge, attitudes and standards that will determine his personality. Children are capable of pulling together the basic Christian ideas and impressions to which they have been exposed into a fairly cohesive, though simple, world-view. The task of Christian instruction during this

period is to help them in this process. It has to be relevant
to their experience of life, to their interests and curiosity,
to the secular knowledge they are acquiring at school, to
the human relations they are developing. In other words,
the Christian doctrine taught must become part of their own
thinking and their knowledge of life as a total experience.

I believe that the following themes should be reflected
in the content of instruction in the last elementary grades
of church school:

God the Creator: How much can science tell us about
the origin of our world? How does this fit in with our
Christian faith? Creation of man and theory of evolution.
Man's responsibility in the world created by God. What are
miracles? The future of our world.

Jesus Christ: the Savior, Son of God, Son of Man. All
these terms are familiar to children, but they have to be
made meaningful. Not only the doctrinal aspect of Jesus
Christ, Son of God, second Person of the Holy Trinity, has
to be taught, but also the meaning of Jesus Christ in one's
own personal life. What does Jesus Christ mean for me?
How is my own life different because of Him? I believe
that some attention should be given to the historicity of the
New Testament and its reliability as a historical document.
The concept of church tradition and how valid it is should
be explained. The meaning of salvation should be taught
not in a way that relegates it to an event that took place
2000 years ago, but so that it is real and meaningful in our
life today. What does salvation mean in the life of eleven-
year-old Tommy? Can it interest him? Yet when I saw the
complete fascination with which ten- to twelve-year-old children listened to the record "Jesus Christ Superstar," I realized their readiness, their hunger, to experience the *reality*
of the person of Jesus Christ, even when this reality is
brought to them in an incomplete and distorted way. This
is a real challenge to our teaching.

The Holy Spirit: Children have learned to speak of the
Holy Spirit in prayer, they know the Gospel accounts of
Epiphany and Pentecost. Their idea of the Holy Spirit is

almost unavoidably associated with events in the past, but I believe that by the time they have reached eleven and twelve years old, children are capable of grasping the idea of God the Holy Spirit, and the life-giving power of the Holy Spirit that affects them personally in their own life here and now. One of the crucial themes for this period is learning to understand the *meaning* of sacrament: What are sacraments? What do they do to me? How is my life made different by receiving sacraments? The idea of the Holy Spirit as a real presence within their own experience is important to develop at this point.

The Church: Children have by now a fairly good idea of the church as a building, the church as a gathering, the church as an institution. They have the experience of the Divine Liturgy, of Holy Communion and Confession. At the same time they all experience in daily life the fact that they are a very small minority of Orthodox living in a non-Orthodox society. Many of their friends are not even Christian, many are Jewish, many are agnostics. Their Christian friends and often one of their parents may be Roman Catholic or Protestant. How does all this fit together? Their own experience with people tells them that the Orthodox are no better than others. In private conversations among themselves they sometimes try to puzzle it out and usually come to the conclusion that people believe in many different ways and all ways can be good. In church school and in class they will quite readily say that the Orthodox Church is the one true Church. I think we should face this discrepancy much more frankly and more fully. Our tendency is simply to ignore, at least at the level of this age group, the existence of plurality and division in Christianity, but in reality this amounts to letting the children deal by themselves with the problem of denominationalism in which they find themselves placed, without any assistance from their religious instruction.

Our Life: There are a lot of ideas about life, about happiness and unhappiness, about what is important or not important, about the purpose of life, that our children absorb from their environment. TV commercials constantly identify the concept of happiness with a brand of deodorant, or a brand of cigarettes, or getting slim, or using a certain kind of shampoo. Being attractive is the supreme goal. Family programs that children watch, or the books they read present stories with happy endings, but the happy ending is usually identified with success. The good guy proves stronger than the bad guy; the poor become rich; Tarzan always saves; the Batman arrives on time; justice prevails over injustice. There is nothing wrong with a "happy ending" in itself, and I do not think that the trend in some of the modern children's books to deal with such problems as homosexuality, insanity, parental delinquency, etc., makes wholesome reading for children. I think, however, that it is necessary to inject Christian meaning into the child's understanding of what is happiness, unhappiness, success or failure.

Lives of saints, such as St. John Chrysostom, SS. Cyril and Methodius, the Apostle Peter and the Apostle Paul, provide plenty of material for discussing what is failure and what is success from a Christian point of view.

All children have to face at some time or other the problem of people being ill, or unhappy, or suffering in some way. We can at least teach them that there is always some meaning to suffering. An interesting piece of research in the Gospel text can be carried out if the children look up words that Christ used in healing suffering people. At this point we can present the idea that God created a good world and did not create suffering. The Spirit of Evil brought suffering to our world. God helps us to overcome suffering by turning it into good, by making us better. (See, for example, St. Paul's mention of the "thorn in the flesh," II Cor. 12:7.)

The study of sacraments towards the end of late childhood allows us to present to children many aspects of the meaning of life. For example the study of the sacrament of marriage can give, in a very simple form, new insights into the whole theme of man-woman relationships and sex— about which children have by now acquired from various sources quite a lot of information and ideas. Looking up

Gen. 1:26-30 and Gen. 2:24, the students can find the tasks assigned to man by God: to have dominion over the earth and all created things, to use freely the fruits of the earth, to marry and have children. It can then be pointed out in a discussion how man had misused these gifts. His responsibility of taking care of the world became a selfish domination; the natural use of the fruits of the earth became greediness, and the coming together of two human beings in marriage became self-satisfaction of physical instincts. The study of the rite of the sacrament can show how Christians are helped in establishing the true meaning of a man and a woman coming together in marriage.

Another theme that is usually avoided and in which older children are often deeply interested is that of death. What happens after death? Why do we pray for the dead? Is death a bad thing or no? Why does God let children and young people die? Death should have been mentioned with even younger children, but at this older age their questions are more thoughtful and more critical. We can find answers in church doctrine, but whatever answers we give they will have to stand the test of the children's rather pragmatic realism. Our answers cannot be abstract, they have to make sense in the terms of the child's experience of life.

The Church Worship: I believe that the keynote of liturgical education during late childhood is giving children *something to think about* and *something to do* in connection with church services. Like children of the younger age group, they should be involved as much as possible in active participation: singing in the junior choir, serving as altar boys, reading in church; and they can do this with a greater sense of responsibility. Additional opportunity may be provided by letting them help with the cleaning and the decoration of the church. Girls can be taught to bake prosfora. Some priests have celebrated the Divine Liturgy on special occasions (like a children's retreat) with the children doing all the singing and reading. The older girls baked the prosfora, and the proskomedia was celebrated in the middle of the church so that the children could stand around, watch it and themselves read the names of the people who were being remembered. All the children received Holy Communion.

Much can be done in the classroom to help the students understand the meaning of services and express this meaning through something they make themselves. Familiar prayers—the Lord's Prayer, for example—can be discussed in depth and posters made to illustrate the meaning of each petition. Making banners, models, diagrams, calendars or mobiles, emphasizing the *meaning* of rites and feasts, provide opportunity for children to express their own thinking. Film-making by children—for example, to illustrate the petitions of a litany—can become a very creative form of learning.

We have to take care that such projects do not lose their perspective, that the right proportion between the several elements involved be kept in mind. Whatever is done must really deepen one's understanding of the meaning involved; the work done must be an authentic creative act on the part of the child; the technique and mechanics of the project must not become too time-consuming and complicated.

These late primary grades are a good time to train the children in the use of the Bible and especially the New Testament as a resource book. Learning to know which parts of the Bible are used during the church services they attend, and how to find the appropriate readings, increases their familiarity with the Scriptures.

It is generally recognized that the celebration of church feasts (with the exception of Christmas and Easter) is greatly eroded in our society today. The very sense of festivity in connection with church holy days has to a large extent disappeared. Johnny has not the faintest idea why the fact that Jesus Christ went up on a hill and was seen talking to Moses and Elijah should make him feel festive or happy. Very young children may be made to feel that there is something special about the service because fruit is blessed and distributed in church, but for the older boys and girls this in itself is not exciting enough. Don't they have fruit at home every day anyway? Our first task then is to prepare the children for calendar events, presenting their meaning not simply as a remembrance of an event that took place a long time ago, but from the point of view of why this event is important for *me now.* And this explanation has to stand the test of the youngsters' realistic thinking. The feast of the Meeting of Our Lord in the Temple can be presented as a "meeting point" of the Old Testament and the New, which is of a purely theoretical interest to children. It can be used to deepen their appreciation of old age—of wisdom, loyalty, hopefulness and faithfulness of very aged members of the family—and perhaps be accompanied by a discussion of what very old people contribute to life. Or it may be used to help the children get a deeper understanding of the person of the Theotokos, the young mother who at this moment of rejoicing listened unafraid to the words "a sword will pierce through your own soul also." There are probably other aspects that can be emphasized. Such lessons should be taught ahead of time, so that when the feast day comes, the children know what it means.

Although it is easier to communicate with older children on an intellectual level, it is much more difficult to penetrate into their inner *spiritual and moral life.* Part of the difficulty lies in the fact that, to a certain extent, they have learned by now to conform to the standards expected of them. When they like an adult—a priest, a teacher, an older friend—they will try to please him by giving the right answer and by reacting emotionally in a way that will gain approval. Therefore not all the feelings they express outwardly are really authentic. Yet I feel that children today tend to be more frank than a generation ago.

Older children do not want to show what they feel, partly because adults rarely understand them, and partly because they are not sure themselves of what they think and feel, and especially *why* they feel this way. I remember witnessing the intense emotion of two girls ten and twelve years old during the night their baby brother was born. They were excited and happy and yet they wept. After a sleepless night the older girl was watching the sun rise, all by herself, obviously deeply stirred, yet quite unable to explain just what she was feeling and why.

Another difficulty is that children are less sentimental than adults and have a sense of humor all their own which can exasperate the best intentioned teacher. I remember especially an elderly and not very qualified woman teacher who could be brought to tears by the ironic remarks of an intelligent eleven-year-old boy. The entire class of basically kind and well-behaved children found this tremendously funny. Several years later they still remember what "great fun" they had in this teacher's class. A teacher may be telling a story by which he expects to awaken the children's compassion and awe, but suddenly some unexpected minor detail will appeal to their sense of humor and they will roar with laughter or go into fits of giggles.

It seems to me that at this age we have to "take on trust" the inner spiritual and moral life of our children. We know it is there, we know it functions and grows in its own mysterious way. We have to *respect* it and its workings even when they remain mysterious to us. We can offer nurture through suitable narratives—Biblical, historical, from lives of saints or from modern life—and through questions and discussion which raise issues that help them to get a better perspective and to perceive new points of view. But what they really get out of it very often remains hidden from us.

Because older children have reached a greater degree of maturity and independence, a new important experience can be introduced into their church life. I would call it "experiences in community living." Church summer camps, retreats, pilgrimages offer opportunities to learn through experience in personal relationships and in shared responsibilities. Though the children are still too young to plan and organize such expeditions themselves, they do gain a greater variety and independence of experience when they take part in such projects.

Adolescence: age 13 to 16

By definition adolescence is the period between child-hood and adulthood. The potential intellectual ability reached during this period is equal to that of adults. Adolescents go very rapidly through a period of physical changes which cause awkwardness, self-consciousness and increased emotional instability.

One of the main characteristics of this period is the young people's *sensitivity* and *dissatisfaction.* They are dissatisfied with themselves, with their family, with their own appearance (wherein lies the cause of infatuation with any extreme fashion of the day). They are dissatisfied with their room and will try to decorate it in weird ways. They are dissatisfied with their process of education: textbooks, grades, teachers, examinations. Unless they happen to be the few who have acquired a special talent, a special intellectual interest and ability, they are fed up with the whole process of formal education. They are dissatisfied with adults—parents, teachers, adults in general—"because they don't understand us" and especially "because they don't trust us," without realizing how practically impossible it is for the most loving parents to "trust" the judgment and wisdom of adolescents who are going out into a new and unfamiliar world, of which they have no experience themselves and where the parents have little influence. Nor do adolescents trust their parents and their parents' judgment and opinions. It is unavoidably a period of mutual distrust.

Adolescents go through a period of painful dissatisfaction with their social life too. What used to be fun, is fun no more. Family vacations lose their glamor. Parties waver between stiff and awkward ones, when the youngsters are too shy to be at ease with each other, and extremely rowdy ones, extravagant experiments including drugs, drink and promiscuity, not because adolescents are basically inclined this way, but because they are frantically eager to investigate new ways of behavior. In most happy families adolescents still feel strong family ties, but they are painfully conscious

of the conflict between these old ties and the new social ties
of the teenage culture.

All these traits, though they often seem negative and
painful, are part of a positive process. What adolescents are
trying to do is to discover themselves and to discover the
relationship in which they stand to others—to adults, to
their peers of their own sex as well as of the opposite one.

The discovery of one's own self involves figuring out
"What do I think?" "What do I feel?" and more generally
"Who am I?". When you were small you dreamed of being
a ballerina, or an astronaut, or a champion in sports. Now
you have to prove to yourself and to others who you are.
"Am I really a great singer?" "Can I become an actress of
genius?" "Have I the makings of a great scientist?" "Will
I be a great football player?" This makes you sensitive to
criticism, easily discouraged and yet capable of driving yourself to the limits of your capacities.

Young people discover themselves in the realm of relations with others. It is always a two-way thing. How do
my parents, my teachers, my priest relate to me and how do
I relate to them? The lines of communication are confused
because adults see me not as I am today, almost grown-up,
but as a composite picture of everything I was yesterday, the
day before yesterday, and when I was a small child. This is
a period when the relationship of love between parents and
children is really being tested. If it was a selfless, non-
possessive love on the part of the parents, always rejoicing
in the child's growth, existing within the framework of
values that imposed discipline on parents and children alike,
it can easily survive this period of search and testing. But
this demands patience and understanding.

A new realm of relations becomes very important—relations with the other sex. For years young people have been
speaking of it, watching it on TV, listening to commercials,
reading about it in magazines. But it was always play, not
the real thing. Now, suddenly, it means something quite
different. It has become something *I* feel, something that
hurts *me,* or gives joy to *me.* Of necessity it is a period of
investigation. "Is this the kind of boy I like?" "Is this the

kind of girl I admire?" Of necessity it is a period of trial
and error, of heartbreaking disappointments, of foolish
mistakes and frustrations. Under the best of circumstances
there evolves gradually a more mature understanding of
what one is and what one is looking for, but the process is
full of pitfalls.

Apart from this intensely personal relationship, there is
the importance of relations with one's peers as a group.
"Am I acceptable?" "Do they like me?" "Are they the kind
of group I want to join?" All these questions have to be
solved by the youngster on his or her own. In the "teenage
culture" of today parents have little to do with adolescent
society. Boys and girls have to figure out for themselves
whether the image imposed on them by their group is the
one they really want to assume.

Much of what I have said above was always true of the
adolescent period. Our society today merely provides a setting, a background against which the problems of adolescence
acquire a new poignancy.

The rapid growth of technological civilization during the
last decades has made our children much more knowledgeable, about sex, about social problems, race, crime,
violence, science, technology. They are not more mature
than adolescents used to be, but they know more, even
though they often lack the maturity to digest this knowledge. They live in a period when the so-called "establish-
ment" is more discredited than it has been for a long time.
The rather arrogant patriotism of the "American way of
life" has been violently rejected by their older brothers and
sisters, nor is there much to support national pride when
our society is having to face problems of ecology, crime and
violence. They hear no voice in American statesmanship concerning politics that really appeals to their spiritual yearn-
ings, to their search for truth or to their innate idealism,
no Abraham Lincoln, not even a Winston Churchill, whose
promise of "nothing but blood, toil, and tears" brought
forth unprecedented heroism in the English people.

The breakdown of Christian morality and traditional
family life in American society began with an earlier gen-

eration. It is not strange that the morality imposed by fear of pregnancy and by resulting social ostracism proved to be not very valid. Society has become more lenient; there is the "pill," so why worry? And what concept of the "sacredness of marriage" can young people have, faced as they are by the high number of divorces and broken marriages among the parents of their contemporaries? The period of affluence through which the parents of modern teen agers have lived has deeply influenced their sense of values. Parents attached too much importance to the status given by expensive cars, suburban homes, fancy equipment, etc. Their children reject this culture in theory, though they have never known the meaning of deprivation. Young people are much in evidence today, they can be seen and heard a lot, and the disapproval of the older generation frequently turns into real hostility. Adolescents themselves are ready to return this hostility, and the generation gap widens.

What then is the task of the Church in confronting our adolescents? Basically, the Church has to offer them *meaningful values* that young people can consciously accept of their own free choice at this special level of maturity and insecurity that they have reached. The Church has to give them an image, a taste, of what life should be, of what is holiness, what is truth, faith, loyalty. The Church is where they can find forgiveness, understanding and love when they have done wrong and are confused and mixed-up. Adolescents need "security-in-freedom" according to the expression of Ronald Goldman, who writes:

> Fundamentally, all human beings having to meet new experiences and new pressures feel insecure until they have come to terms with them. This is why adolescence is so insecure a time of development. The stresses to be faced and the adjustments to be made are greater than at any other period of human growth. Just as the adolescent needs freedom to experiment and to explore, he

also needs secure bases from which to go out and
to which he can return.*

What has been up to now the place of adolescents in
our church in the United States? How has the church tried
to reach them? There are some things that our experience
tells us are not very effective. Large mass youth organiza-
tions, based on ethnic origin, providing opportunities for
social life and superficial acknowledgement of loyalty to
the Orthodox Church, do not seem to appeal to the majority
of Orthodox adolescents today, though most of these organ-
izations came into existence as youth movements 30, 40 or 50
years ago and were quite spontaneous in their time. Nor
does the Sunday School movement answer their needs, for
adolescents thoroughly dislike being formally part of a
children's program.

Our adolescents need urgently two aspects of religious
education in order to help them gain maturity. They need
the opportunity to make religion a part of their own experience of life, of their own thinking, of their own motivation, through very informal free discussions, through participation in church work, through friendships. They also
need to acquire information that will allow them to think
intelligently, that will provide some material for evalua-
tion and judgment. You cannot think profitably of something about which you know practically nothing, and we
have to admit that this is the status of a large majority of
adolescents. They know very little about Christianity at the
level of maturity they have attained. In order to be helpful
and creative, any youth group must combine freedom and
spontaneity of expression with an exposure to information
about the Christian faith that will enrich their thinking.

All the teaching they need to acquire about the Bible
and about the Church will be better assimilated if they feel
a need for it. Thus teaching should be structured around
questions and problems that are real to young people. The
information must be presented as a means of finding answers. This kind of approach is very demanding on the

---

*Readiness for Religion, p. 166.

leader, not only because he must be well informed, and know where he can find information, but also because he must be flexible and sensitive to what takes place in the students' minds.

I hesitate to outline a course of studies for senior adolescents, for the very reason that such a course should be built around the abilities of the leader and the interests of this particular group. Basically adolescents need information in the same areas that shaped our curriculum for younger grades—doctrine, liturgics, Bible study, church history, spirituality and ethics; but the most effective way of communicating the knowledge is determined by circumstances. A youth choir with a good leader may provide excellent opportunities for instruction if the leader makes sure that at every rehearsal there is a brief explanation of the meaning of the words, the liturgical placement of the hymns and of the meaning of the feast. If in addition to this he is able to establish an atmosphere of friendliness, of concern and interest in each member of the group, we have an ideal teaching situation. Similar groups can be created for junior church school teachers or teachers' assistants when, in preparing lessons for very young children, they will have to make sure that they understand the content, the purpose and meaning of each lesson. Training groups for senior altar boys or summer camp counsellors are also very useful. Learning to paint icons is another possibility.

If a regular academic class or study group is planned, a good general principle is to start with asking a few questions that will catch the interest of the group, questions like "How are Orthodox Christians different from other Christians?" "Do I really want to be Orthodox?" "Why?" "What do I like about other faiths?" "What do I feel difficult to accept in the Orthodox faith?" This stage of the work should help to establish an atmosphere of mutual trust and freedom in expressing one's opinions. The young people should not feel that the leader wants them to give the *right* answers, but that he is genuinely interested in finding out what they think. Sometimes it is easier to get frank statements when the answers to the questions are given in writing, anonymously. Answering such a questionnaire may take up a full first session.

In discussing the answers given and the additional questions asked one should have a variety of resources. One can begin with historical information that can explain the background of the Church as it is today. There can be sessions on the liturgical aspects of other Christian and non-Christian faiths as compared to our Church. A study of the life of some saint or great person may be helpful. It is very helpful when such studies are not merely book-work but involve visits, interviews, research and reports by individual students. Thus the course would involve open discussions, lectures, book research done by students and outside activities.

Younger teenagers can still be interested in activities such as poster-making, or making a film, or producing a newspaper tied in with some past time in church or biblical history, but these must not be gimmicks to keep the students busy. The important thing is that anything the students do must be an effort to express an idea, discover a meaning.

Another type of work that is helpful for their growth as members of the Church is any work that involves relations with others and responsibility on the part of the students: organizing a "march" on behalf of some service; planning, organizing and carrying out a pilgrimage or a retreat; planning a special church celebration of some event, etc.

Most important of all is the kind of relationship that is established between the adult leader—whether priest or lay person—and the young people. The leader should earn their trust as a friend, with understanding and sympathy, yet with firmness in his own convictions and genuine interest in the person of the adolescent. This is what the young people are really looking for: a friend, whose honesty they trust, who really accepts them as they are, and who, they feel, is in possession of some convictions and traits that are relevant to their needs. Our greatest problem is to find such leaders.

CHAPTER III

Christian Education in the Family

From earliest times it has been understood that the
Christian education of children should be carried on chiefly
within the home, within the family. Instruction given in
church schools and attendance of church services are very
important, but dependant, of course, on the family's cooperation and attitude. This function of the family (send-
ing the children to church school and bringing them to
church) is only supplementary, however, to the basic process
of Christian education that goes on, day after day, within
the home. There is a curious lack of helpful material on
the Christian education of children at home. In the rich
treasury of church writings and liturgical texts there is little
appreciation of parental work and little empathy for it. The
sermons addressed to parents are almost always rather general condemnations of parental indifference to church duties
or appeals to be conscientious about bringing children to
church. Even when the Church deals with specific situations, such as prayers for a mother who has given birth to
a child, the prayers of churching, and prayer for a mother
who has had a miscarriage, there seems to be a strange lack
of insight into the spiritual needs and feelings of a mother.
The rule forbidding a mother to attend church services and
receive Holy Communion for six weeks after childbirth is
difficult to understand.*

*See "Liturgical Notes," by Father Zheludkov, published in the Russian-
language periodical *Vestnik russkogo Khristianskogo dvizheniya,* No. 106
(Paris, 1973).

Yet the family is recognized as the "home church," and the task of the parents is really a kind of lay priesthood. Within a Christian family our Christian faith must be incarnated; it must be brought to life in the daily, hourly experience of living. Children attend church school for an hour a week; they attend church services for another hour or two, but family life goes on all the time, every day of the year, and is embodied in every detail of living—in personal relationships, in providing, preparing and partaking of food, in health and in sickness. It is the environment within which the life of the child unfolds.

I cannot attempt to outline a program of how the Church can guide the family and help it. At best we can attempt here to gain a slightly better understanding of just what is the Christian growth that takes place in the family and what are the problems and the educational tasks involved.

Love in Family Life

The essential nature of a family is that it is based on love, is an embodiment of love between several human beings. A family is not made by legal definition; it is not characterized by similarity of ages, or occupations, or tastes, or by the number of people within the group. It is based on the love of husband and wife for each other and the love between parents and children. The experience of family love is different from other expressions of love. It is existential in the sense that—unlike romantic love or devotion to some cause, that demand proclamation and explanation in words—family love does not have to be consciously verbalized. Furthermore, it is a universal experience, because every human being belongs to some kind of family.

The Christian concept of a family and of family love has a special character. It is akin to the trinitarian concept of God: a human being cannot exist completely by itself. It becomes fully human within a relationship of love with other human beings. Such a relationship can be violated—human mates *may* not love each other, parents *may* not love their children, children *may* not love their parents—but lack of love is always a violation of the true nature of the family.

Husband and wife relationship

The husband-wife relationship is very different from the romantic period of "being in love," which serves as a kind of big wave to lift the boat off the sand. In the husband-wife relationship each one of the partners gives up his or her "selfness." One person becomes only a part of a new unity. In order to be happy, both of them have to be happy; if one is unhappy, both are. No decision can be an isolated one. The hurts of the other mate mean as much as your own hurts. Whatever you do, the other one is involved. In a very real sense in marriage two become one.

The difficulty of the relationship is that *loving* is not the same as *liking*. There are always traits and qualities that a couple dislikes within each other. It may be arrogance or laziness, talkativeness or impatience, some habits and tastes inherited from one's former family, some superficial mannerisms. There are circumstances in which a husband and a wife simply get on each other's nerves. How does one then deal in love with traits one dislikes? This abrasive nature of the married life is what one might call its "askesis," and I have heard experienced monks say that the ascetic effort of married life is greater than that of a monk in a monastic community. In other social groups you can avoid a person who has irritating traits. You can control yourself and put up with another's exasperating traits for a limited time; but in a family there is no way of isolating yourself. Such as you are, you have to come to terms with the other members of your family as they are. A Christian family (the "home Church") comes into being only when the "coming to terms" is a true incarnation of Christian faith, hope and love.

Chapter 13 of the First Epistle to the Corinthians re-

mains forever the most helpful and practical manual of love
in human relationships: "love is patient and kind; love is
not jealous or boastful; it is not arrogant or rude. Love does
not insist on its own way; it is not irritable or resentful; it
does not rejoice at wrong, but rejoices in the right. Love
bears all things, believes all things, endures all things . . ."
The effort to apply this kind of love, the constant effort
to deal in this spirit with the thousands of aggravating difficulties in our daily relations goes on throughout the long
years of every Christian marriage.

I am convinced that love does not exclude anger. Something is wrong with your love if you are never angry.
Precisely because a husband or a wife has a lover's vision
of his or her mate as a person who is worth loving, anything
that destroys this vision cannot leave that person indif-
ferent. Jesus got angry at the people who sold things in
the Temple precisely because He loved them. Anger rooted
in love is a necessary element in husband-wife relationships;
marriage is not a "society of mutual admiration." I would
go even further and say that there is nothing wrong in a
certain fear of one's mate's anger. In a sense husband and
wife become each other's conscience. But anger is not resentment, nor is it irritability. Anger flares up quickly and
then comes reconciliation, forgiveness and compassion for
the one who is hurt.

Parental love

As family life progresses, it gains a new dimension and
a new perspective. If marriage involved giving up one's
singleness, each spouse becoming a part of the other one,
then with the arrival of children parents find themselves
giving up more and more of themselves and sometimes feel
lost in the whirlpool of family preoccupations and duties.
In this process each member of the family has to find his
or her own new personality, a stronger and richer one.
"Unless a grain of wheat falls into the earth and dies, it
remains alone, but if it dies it bears much fruit" (John

12:24). This true "askesis" of family life is a difficult and painful process. The "self" of each member is constantly squeezed, abrased, trodden upon because of the needs of the others. And this effort has to be made whether you are supported by your Christian faith or not. Broken nights, physical exhaustion, limitations of one's freedom, worry cannot be avoided. The father may feel neglected because his wife becomes more mother than wife. This violation of "self" can be resented and cause much bitterness. In terms of Christian faith, a willing sacrifice of one's swollen sense of "selfness," or self-importance, can become the sacrifice from which a new and bigger person is born. Parallel to the willingness to sacrifice something of oneself, there has to be an equally willing effort to recognize the "self" of others, to understand their personalities, their points of view and their gifts.

Parents need enlightenment and guidance in understanding the meaning of their relationship with their children. The basis of this relationship is a responsible love, which includes authority and respect and understanding for the child's personality. From a Christian point of view parental love has all the emotional richness of love, but it must not be possessive. At its best it is completely unselfish, its model given to us by the love of Mary the Theotokos for her Son. Parental love should not be felt by the parent as a *gift* given to the child, for which he can expect gratitude. Every time I hear parents complain that their children are ungrateful, I have doubts about the quality of their parental love. A mother's love for her child fills her own life, enriches it. It is felt as a love for something bigger than herself, that does not belong to her in the sense of ownership. Children have to grow *away* from their parents. The sacrificial or Christian meaning of parental love is precisely the acceptance of this, a joyful acceptance of the children's growth into independence. The image of Abraham and Isaac still has a meaning for every parent today in the sense that a parent is willing to offer the life of the child to God, not to end his life but so that his life may be lived under God rather than under the parent. I always feel that this is well illustrated by the icons of the Theotokos where Jesus is represented as sitting straight up in her lap, her arms surrounding Him, but not "clutching" Him.

Children's love of parents and siblings

The difficulty involved in the changing love of children for parents is that it is part of a process of growing away from the parents. The total dependence of early childhood, the complete reliance and confidence in parental omnipotence, is very important and satisfying for parents. But a child's normal development takes him through stages of growth, of independence and rebellion. Under the best of circumstances relationships of friendship and mutual respect eventually are established; and gradually these change into the compassionate, understanding and grateful love of adult children for elderly parents.

The love-hate relationship between brothers and sisters is, in a sense, a pattern of our relationships with all human beings. Affection and love between brothers and sisters is often taken for granted. To a certain degree this is justified, but we all know the violence of the opposite feelings among siblings. Children who are genuinely fond of each other and have a strong feeling of belonging to one family, will fight with complete abandon. They will frequently say, and mean it at the moment, "I hate him..." "I'll kill her..." "I'll never speak to him again..." In a sense all this is very superficial and natural and is almost part of the growing up in a family. It is normal for a growing child to experience anger at others, just as it is normal for an infant to scream when it is hungry. Many parents say "It's good for them to get it out of their system!" and there is a certain wisdom in this attitude, because simply repressing one's anger and never showing it is probably more unwholesome than a good clean fight or a violent quarrel, after which all is forgotten and forgiven.

Yet there is another side to it. A young baby's screaming may be a symptom of hunger. The mother tries to feed it on time, to establish some kind of schedule, so that the screaming is not normally necessary. If quarrels and anger are symptoms of inner needs, these needs must be recognized and dealt with. If the purpose of the fight is to "get it out of your system," then it is important to make sure that this something *is* "gotten out," is recognized and understood by the parent or the adult in charge, and the child is gradually helped to deal with it. Anger is a way of saying that something in my relationship with another person does not satisfy my wants. I want this toy, this chair, this cup, this person, this approval to be *mine,* and he has taken it! It is a conflict in the desire to possess. It may be a way of obtaining love: "I hit him because he would not speak to me!" It may be an inability to solve a problem, the problem of being too young, or too old, or not smart enough, or too smart, or not popular enough. It may be a form of jealousy. It may be an effort to determine one's own position, one's own role, to determine "who's the boss."

Problems like these and endless similar ones will be with us all our life. The purpose of education, especially Christian education, is to help a person grow up and mature, to help him adopt a creative, constructive and "good" way of dealing with these problems. The old principle "you learn what you practice" remains true. A well established habit of dealing with problems by getting angry at another person may lead a child to become the infantile type of adult who loses his temper at the slightest provocation.

In handling children's quarrels and fights a parent should first of all recognize them as symptoms. Repressing symptoms does not really help, though obviously a measure of self-control must be taught: one cannot allow children to hurt each other or to make life intolerable for all around. Symptoms are a wholesome thing if they help us to recognize and deal with the cause. Many causes of anger, such as frustration at not being recognized or inability to do something, are properly and adequately dealt with in the normal process of growing up in a basically secure and loving family. But this process of growing up and maturing can be encouraged and helped. It does help to "cool" a quarrel, to separate the

fighters, to have each one separately tell you without interruptions what happened and why. Usually in the very process
of trying to present the conflict in words, unthreatened by
interruptions and arguments, the emotion of anger subsides,
the quarrel is ended and made up without any formal
apologies. More than this, occasionally it gives to the one
who tells as well as to the one who listens calmly an insight into the real cause of the anger: jealousy, or loneliness, or a feeling of rejection, or whatever it may be. This
provides the opportunity for the parent to help the child
gain understanding of himself and of his place within the
family and his life. "Yes, you are the youngest, and being
youngest means this and that . . ." "Yes, you are a girl, and
this means that you can do some things no boy can . . ."
"Because you are the oldest, this and that is difficult, but
then . . ."

On the other hand, children's anger and their quarrels
can draw the parents attention to some conditions that
cause them, and these should be dealt with by the parents.
A child that feels rejected has to be given more attention;
his sense of inferiority can be relieved by discovering and
recognizing his gifts and abilities that have been ignored.
A "bossy" child may need to be given more responsibilities.

I strongly believe that most of this can be done, and
should be done, through actions and attitudes rather than
with words. Preaching at children does very little good;
as a matter of fact, it can do harm when it teaches them
to conceal real motives and emotions with words that do
not really correspond to them.

The basic aim of Christian education within the family
is to convey to children the concept of what is good and
what it means to feel good. This "good" means the condition of blessedness, joy, inner peace and love for others.
It is reflected in Peter's words on the day of Transfiguration: "It is good for us to be here!" If the children have
in their home the basic desire to be good and have really
experienced what it means "to feel good," a solid foundation has been laid for their Christian growth.

The larger family

The trend in our society today is to have the family reduced to the parents-children unit. There is probably not much that an individual family can do about this, but at least it can recognize the importance of the larger family group in a Christian home. For younger children, their family and their home is their world. Their relationships with their parents are unavoidably of a rather selfish nature: the parents are the providers of all things; the parents are the power that regulates their life. Generally speaking, children are the center around which the parents' life revolves. On the other hand, relationships with grandparents, aunts, uncles and cousins are generally of a much more relaxed nature. There is a bond of affection, of mutual belonging, but it is looser. Differences in living are more pronounced. For children this provides a great opportunity for new experiences in relationships. An uncle may be an original, whose way of life is very different from that of the parents; a grandmother or a great-grandmother may be an invalid whose needs demand greater attention than the children's, etc. Though the day of the large family clan is over, we should at least make an effort to maintain family relationships through memory, through correspondence, through visits and through family celebrations. There is still a place for the family album. Affectionate relationships within the "larger family" are a very wholesome transitional experience leading from the small family ties into membership in society as a whole.

The family world-view

One of the most important aspects of family life is a common understanding of life, of the purpose of life, of happiness, of the "hierarchy of life values"—in other words, of all that makes up one's world-view. I believe that this is not just a question of a common faith or a common ideology but something more mysterious and deep-going.

A common understanding is difficult to attain in the case of "mixed marriages," but very often it is quite absent even when husband and wife are formally of the same faith. On the other hand, I have seen married couples who truly realized a union of love in their marriage and whose "oneness," or common vision of life, somehow included accepting one another's differences.

Basically a common vision of life is built on a common concept of happiness, and in a Christian family it means a Christian concept of happiness. The desire to be happy is ingrained in the human being. Many of the anti-Christian influences that surround us are an appeal to the human desire for happiness. Every ad we see in the subway promises some kind of happiness and peace of mind if only we buy this, or do that (even "attend a church of your choice"). The longing for happiness, the instinctive feeling that it is a desirable state of life and that when we are unhappy we have broken away from that which is intended for us, seems to be inborn in man. Perhaps it is a kind of subconscious memory of the human condition before the Fall.

This theme was very well treated by the late Bishop Sergius of Prague in his series of lectures on "Well-Being."* After speaking of the human nostalgia for happiness, he goes on to say that we feel *unhappy* when we accept the temporary possession of ourselves by the power of evil as our real self, reflecting the true nature of our personality. In other words we become unhappy when we *accept evil as an authentic part of our real self*. This confusion causes us to speak and think wrongly. In our relationship with others we also tend to identify their true nature and character with the evil we see in them, and we react to this evil as if it were an organic part of their natural personality, as if they themselves were evil. Everyday life, and especially family life, is a means of reaching for the *real* person, establishing relations with the *real* person and refusing to accept that which is unreal, temporary and evil as part of the essential nature of the person we love. Every day of our life is given

*"O Blagobytii," published in the magazine *Vechnoye* (Paris, Jan. 1954).

to us for finding at least a particle of that goodness and joy which are the essence of eternal life. In this search for the goodness of life we have to be creative in the way we approach every moment of our life. Such a creative over-coming of obsession with evil leads to a joyful perception of the world. In overcoming sin we reveal good, and in revealing good, we participate in eternal life. As a method of overcoming evil, Bishop Sergius suggests training oneself in the perception of goodness in people and goodness in life.

I have cited Bishop Sergius rather extensively because I found his approach so particularly relevant to the task of establishing a Christian family way of life and because it shows a real insight into its problems. This approach applies to the mutual (and often "justified") exasperation so often felt by husband and wife; to the parents' dissatisfaction with the tastes, attitudes and development of their children; to the children's antagonism toward their parents and toward each other. It pin-points the true difference between a "happy" and an "unhappy" family.

The Christian understanding of happiness as a "blessed state," like that described in the Beatitudes, needs to be taught to parents and in turn to be taught—and exem-plified—by them. Fundamentally blessedness is a state of love and of loving communication, a sense of trust (which in secular terms we replace by the word "security"), and the freedom to grow and fulfill one's God-given creative gifts (in the sense of the Genesis account of creation). Unfortunately the idea of Christianity held by many lay persons is lacking often this sense of joy and blessedness, and instead Christianity is identified with a rather formal set of duties.

It seems to me that the most urgent task in the Chris-tian education of parents is not so much to emphasize their duties in observing church rules, in making their children attend church school, etc., but in unfolding to them the *meaning* of the basic realities of life. Only when parents begin to ask themselves such basic questions as "What is happiness?" "What is sin?" "What does it do to us?" "What

is love?" "What do my children mean to me?" "What do
I want for them?", will they begin to perceive the true nature
of their duties and obligations. Observing rules is important
and laws must not be neglected, but first the parents must
be motivated by an insight into the meaning of life.

Family discipline

Discipline, "the cross of authority," is another aspect of
love that must be borne by the parents. In the family, discipline means, first of all and most of all, an authentic recognition of the whole order and structure of discipline and obedience within which the family lives. This includes both the
wife's obedience to her husband (which, it seems to me, is
much harder on the husband than on the wife, and most often
it is the husband who fails to assume this discipline) and
the husband's consideration of and respect for his wife (I
Peter 3). It also includes the principle of the hierarchy of
obedience. There may be disagreements when the husband
or the wife feels that the values involved are higher than
the harmony of their relationships: it may be a matter of
principles and convictions that cannot be given up; it may
be, for example, that the attitude of one of the parents is
destroying the children's personalities. But whenever obedience is to be breached, it has to be done for the sake of a
higher obedience.

Children are quick to recognize the validity of the obedience and discipline which parents accept for themselves—
whether it is faithfully attending church, not cheating on
telephone or bus fares, or showing kindness and hospitality
to guests, or controlling habits like smoking or drinking.
Obedience to law as a principle of action, not as a formal
ritual, not as lip service, is one of the foundations of the
Christian home. The obedience of children grows within this
framework.

Training in obedience begins with very young children
who have to be protected against hazards that they do not
understand. "Don't run into the street!" "Don't touch!"

"Don't climb on this!" It often involves physical restriction of the child's action. The wise parent will always avoid demanding obedience from a very young child when it cannot be enforced—for instance "giving a kiss" when the child does not want to do it. Very soon, however, the child's obedience becomes a matter of free choice: "Mummy said not to do this. But what if I do?"

It is at this point that the general atmosphere of obedience in the home becomes important. There must be no confusion: forbidden things are clearly forbidden, punishments are consistent and not haphazard, and the hierarchy of values must also be clear. When a child's disobedience causes some minor disaster, he should be scolded or punished for the disobedience. But a similar disaster—things broken, bathroom flooded, etc.—caused by awkwardness, or desire to help, is not a matter for punishment or scolding. An old nurse who spent all her life looking after children spoke of two families in which she had been employed: " In the X. home everything was forbidden, but as a matter of fact, you could do anything you wanted. In the Y. home you could do anything you wanted, but what was forbidden was really forbidden."

As children grow older this insight into the hierarchy of obedience becomes more and more important. Christian parents can help their children realize that the motivation behind all discipline and all obedience is "Thy will be done" and not "my will be done."

Ideally there should be a clear and firm structure of discipline accompanied by a living insight into the child's motivation, but not weakened by fear of being unpopular.

It is important at this point to underscore the difference between the clear recognition of discipline and obedience to rules and the imposition by parents of their tastes, emotions, moods and feelings. It may be a perfectly valid rule that TV is not watched on Holy Friday, but whether a boy or a girl feels the emotion or mood which is quite sincerely experienced by the parents is another matter. You cannot demand it, you cannot prescribe it. You can only hope that some day, in his own good time, your youngster will discover it for himself. In many priests' families, for example, we find children who at one or another stage of their development express animosity against religious concepts and religious feelings simply because they have been "over-fed" with religious talk. An artist's child may seek release in a complete and total absorption in sports. An emotionally tense and idealistic mother may be unable to reach her daughter, who is absorbed in her appearance, her clothes and her social life. Attitudes and emotions cannot be forced upon a youngster by endlessly explaining them, or by expecting him to react emotionally in the ways we wish.

Summing up the theme of obedience and discipline in the home, I feel that the major requirements are:

A general structure of obedience and discipline within which the entire family, including the parents, lives.

Clear-cut, simple rules of obedience, established by the parents and fortified by the parents' acceptance of the burden of this constant and continuous responsibility.

A loving insight into the child's motivation, an understanding of his point of view, his tastes and his personality.

A very clear understanding of what can be expected from and imposed by discipline and what is outside its province and should not be imposed by authority.

Worship in the home

The real question is whether prayer can be *taught*. Prayer is a relationship with God, it is like "standing before God" and can only come from a person's own sincere effort, helped by the grace of God. In some ways learning to pray can be compared to learning to talk. There has to be an inborn capacity for speech; there must be some content that the speaker wishes to convey; but there also has to be training and exercise in the process of speaking. Just as the family is the natural place for learning to speak and for establishing communication in words between the little child and other members of the family, so also is the family the place where a child can naturally be involved in "learning to pray." From participation in the prayer of others, from the habit acquired in daily routine, prayer can become a real experience, a childish experience at first, but growing into an authentic adult experience later. I am giving this general definition of prayer because it is quite important for parents to realize what they are trying to do: memorizing prayers, though necessary in many ways, is not really teaching the child to pray.

The best way for parents to introduce their children to the experience of prayer is to share with them their own experience of prayer. It begins with the parents' prayer over a quite young infant, which is probably one of the most prayerful experiences a mother can have. This can become the foundation of a child's daily experience of prayer.

The usual first verbal prayer of young children is the "God bless . . ." kind, in which the child makes up a whole list of names of people he wants to mention. It is very important that the parent really pray with the child. It is important for the child to have this first experience of *speaking to God.* In this way he participates in the affirmation *that God is,* and it is important for him to put into this something of his own—the listing of the people he knows and loves. The sense of the presence of God comes quite naturally at this age. As the child gets older, the "Thank you, God, . . ." prayers can be added, and the parent can help the child to remember the especially enjoyable events of the day.

The first "learned" prayer in most Orthodox families is probably the formula "In the name of the Father and of the Son and of the Holy Spirit, Amen," used when making the sign of the cross. It involves movement which the little child accepts as a kind of finger-play; it is short; it has a meaning valid for adults also, that will not have to be unlearned later. In this sense I believe it is better than made-up "children's" prayers like "Now I lay me down to sleep...," which are not really the children's own and involve memorizing something that later will seem childish to them.

It is more difficult to find the best approach for longer prayers. To ignore the treasury of prayers of great saints that we find in our prayer books seems unreasonable, rather like restricting ourselves to baby-talk when we speak to growing children. Yet anyone who has listened to a mumbled, lightning-quick recital of the Lord's Prayer by an eight- or nine-year-old ("and lead us not into Penn Station...") will have doubts about whether this is really learning to pray.

One approach is to have the children say just one sentence at a time of a formal prayer, making sure they really understood it. A prayer can be explained in general terms ("This is a prayer to God the Holy Spirit, who gives us life..."). The children will then learn to say just one brief sentence: "O Heavenly King, the Comforter, come and abide [live] in us!" Gradually during the year the sentence can be completed and filled out, and the whole prayer can become familiar and meaningful. This also applies to prayers before great feasts: we can use at first just the key-sentence, or the first words, that will allow the children to recognize the hymn in church.

Prayer time, however short, must be a time of unhurried, relaxed communication between parent and child. To observe this rule is one of the most difficult tasks a parent can have, but it is well worth the effort. Ten minutes are enough to read or tell a short Bible story, to talk about a verse of prayer, or about some problem or event of the day. I believe that the most important thing parents can do in teaching their children to pray is to have a daily brief time of unhurried communication with their young children, and to inject into this time the habit of prayer, the habit of "standing before God." For practical reasons it seems easier to have the longer period of prayer at bedtime and a very short one—perhaps simply making the sign of the cross and asking God's blessing for the day—in the morning, when the children can do it individually, on their own.

Besides morning and evening prayer, there are a number of other occasions for worship at home. Meal-time prayers are now often squeezed out of family life because meal-time as such—meals as a more or less formal family gathering—has disappeared. Breakfast, as a matter of course, often means snatching something as various members of the family rush off to school or work; at lunch-time most families do not come home, and at dinner-time parents are glad to let the children settle down with their plates in front of the TV. It is useless to bewail or decry these circumstances, but I think that all families should make an effort to maintain the tradition of the family meal whenever possible, at least on Sundays or special occasions. Traditions regarding meal-time prayers vary: in some families it is simply making the sign of the cross, in others it may be reading a prayer, or singing one. What matters is having this short instant of pulling ourselves together, of giving recognition to the presence of God in our life.

Another occasion for family prayers is when someone goes away on a trip. A Russian custom is for the whole family to sit down for a moment of silence, ending it by making the sign of the cross. In general, making the sign of the cross to bless someone is a good, short, silent way of prayer. There are certainly many opportunities when parents would do well to give this quick blessing to their son or daughter. And singing "God grant you many years!" can be suitably added to any birthday, namesday or anniversary celebration.

All aspects of family life have to stand the rather exacting test of authenticity. Only that custom will survive which is simple, sincere and unpretentious. Family prayers are no exception to this rule, but it is vital for a Christian family to find a form of daily acknowledgment of the presence of God in our life.

Celebration of feasts

Another aspect of church life is closely tied with family worship. Home traditions tied in with liturgical feasts and fasts are vital for Christian education. The festive character of church feasts, that which makes them a real celebration for children, is maintained when it is reflected in their experience of celebration at home. Only the home can provide the children with actual experience of having fun, of rejoicing because it is a feast day. Liturgically the feast takes place in church, verbal explanation of its meaning can be given in church school, but to make it a feast for children it must be celebrated at home. Probably it is for this very reason that we notice such a decline in the celebration of church feasts. In the agricultural communities of the old world most of the church feasts were tied in with the whole way of life. I can still remember many traditions observed in my own childhood—the decoration of homes with green boughs at Pentecost, the blessing of the first ripe fruit on Transfiguration Day, setting birds free on Annunciation Day, the pancakes and sleigh-rides of "Butter Week" (last week before Great Lent), the fun of the "pussy-willow fair" on Palm Sunday. Today we still have traditions that are part of our life-style: Thanksgiving Day dinner, the Christmas tree and gifts at Christmas time, blessing of water and homes at Epiphany, food restrictions during Great Lent, preparation of food for Easter and breaking the fast on Easter night, the Serbian tradition of the "Slava," the Greek "Vasilopita." Orthodoxy in America must treasure such traditions and build up its own rich and meaningful ones, as appropriate to its needs as were the traditions of the "old countries" in centuries past. This is a good way to overcome the anemia of our church life.

This task is a real challenge to individual families and parents. I heard about two incidents when grandmothers showed real ingenuity. A Greek grandmother, troubled because there was no vigil light in her children's home and concerned about preserving the light of the Easter night candle that she had brought back from church, blew out and then re-lit the pilot light of the kitchen gas range with the Easter flame. Another grandmother was puzzled how to bring to her grandchildren the festive spirit of the Nativity of Theotokos. The children's parents were at work; the children themselves were in school; no one except the grandparents had attended church. By the time the children were to come home, the grandmother had replaced the icon in the kitchen corner by one of the Theotokos, lit a vigil light in front of it and made a big birthday cake, which she placed on the kitchen table. Surprized, the children asked whose birthday it was, and the occasion became a real celebration.

The family's responsibility in Christian instruction

A Christian family cannot shirk its responsibility for conveying to children a certain amount of information and knowledge about their faith. This applies first of all to the younger children, who should be exposed at home to basic ideas about God, about Jesus Christ's life on earth, about prayer and church worship, about feasts and great saints. Many parents need help in this task. They need the information themselves and they need to realize how important it is for their children. They also have to learn to distinguish between what is basic truth, the essence of our Christian Orthodox faith, and what are secondary traditions accumulated by popular piety (like "not cutting on Sunday"). There is nothing wrong about such traditions, but they may be harmful when they are given primary, almost superstitious importance. I would say that the Christian information the family must convey consists basically of ideas about God: His presence, His power, His love, His care, His justice; familiarity with a number of Bible stories, especially New Testament ones; a few simple church prayers; a very elementary knowledge of the church services which the family attends; an elementary understanding of major feasts, at least of the Nativity of Our Lord, Epiphany, Palm Sunday, Holy Week, Pascha, Pentecost.

More important, especially as the children grow older, is the parents' interest in stimulating the children's desire to learn more. Parents cannot know everything, but they can show their interest, their curiosity, their desire to find out. Unplanned conversations that come up at unexpected moments in response to a child's sudden question, in reaction to a trying or upsetting situation, are a very important means of education. I believe that parents should overcome their tendency to feel that they are expected to know everything and to answer all questions. They will really do more good if they share with their children the desire to find answers to questions, to think through problems. The parish priest cannot give all the answers either, and it seems to me that the most "growth-encouraging" attitude is to stimulate the children's desire to "find out," to look for information: "Seek and you will find, knock and it will be opened to you" (Matt. 7:7).

To summarize: In order to be truly Christian, a family has to accept life, its values and its challenges, in the spirit of the Christian faith; and this does not always coincide with the nominal piety of the parents. A Christian family constantly must endeavor to establish relationships of love within the family and with those outside the family, on the basis of the kind of love described in I Corinthians chap. 13. A Christian family must live within a framework of discipline recognized by all its members, and within a hierarchy of Christian values. In a Christian family the daily routine of life must be penetrated by the light of the recognition of God's presence—in family worship and in church traditions and celebrations. In a Christian home the growth of the children's minds, talents and gifts must be stimulated and cherished in the spirit of the Christian understanding of the great value of human personality.

CHAPTER IV

The Church School

The limited task of the church school

There was a time when a good church school system was believed to be a cure-all for Christian education. This belief made itself felt even in the type of church buildings constructed in our parishes. Some sixty years ago a church building was a temple, a place of worship with, at best, a basement hall for social activities and banquets. Twenty years ago every new parish was especially proud of its educational facilities, often a separate school building with sound-proof classrooms and excellent equipment. Certainly no teacher today wants to go back to teaching five or six classes in the deafening noise of the single church hall, but there is also a growing awareness that instruction given in the church school is not a panacea. The lessons taught are not reflected in the home life of the children, nor do the very real concerns and issues of family life find any interpretation and echo in the lessons taught. The liturgical life of the parish often does not embody what is taught in the textbooks. Lenten services, Vespers, Matins, the sacrament of Anointing with Oil, and sometimes even the sacrament of Confession may never be part of the children's experience. Furthermore, textbook instruction has little relevance to the real life experience of the child. Textbooks are based on adult thinking, and even when an effort is made to use the children's vocabulary, the ideas presented are far

removed from the children's authentic interests and thoughts.
Trends within non-Orthodox religious educational movements reflect a growing conviction that intellectual instruction of children in matters of faith is simply useless, because
it becomes distorted in the child's mind through misunder-
standing and will be useless as a basis for later adult
concepts.

I believe that such a sweeping condemnation of church
school instruction is exaggerated. Obviously the images children conceive of the religious ideas we try to teach them
are very different from our own. We may say "God made
the world" and a five-year-old may visualize God sitting
down and modeling figures of animals like clay toys. But
are not our own concepts of God and of God's actions also
very much removed from the reality of God? Do we really
know God? Yet every Christian at every stage, in his own
limited way tries to confess his faith in God. Children do
not speak like adults, yet we do not consider this a reason
not to expose them to adult speech until the time they can
enunciate properly. This is an essential part of Orthodox
teaching and is based on Christ's own attitude toward little
children, His recognition of the *validity* of their religious
experience. The belief in the validity of the child's perception of religious reality is basic in our Church tradition of
sacraments received by young children. If we accept the
correctness of giving sacraments to children, we have to
accept the need for some form of verbal explanation of
them. We can progress gradually in speaking, for example,
of Holy Communion: "Something good to eat," "Holy
Food," "Food of Jesus Christ," "when you receive Holy
Communion, you receive Jesus Christ in your life," and so
on; and at each stage of the progression, the statement is
true and not something to be unlearned later.

At each stage of growth a child has his own capacity
for experiencing a relationship with God, and this capacity
can be nurtured and strengthened when we share with the
child our own experience of life with God. Such a sharing,
transcending intellectual rationalizations, is the essence of
the life of the Church and should be the essence of church

school teaching. We should certainly prune our manuals and lessons, eliminating verbalizations and thought-structures that are in fact meaningless for children; but whatever comes within the experience of children—birth, death, prayer, sin, forgiveness, love, God's action and presence in life—should be part of what we talk about to children at the level of maturity that they have reached.

I am convinced that church school instruction is very useful and important for the Christian education of children, but we have to recognize clearly both its goals and its limitations.

The objectives of church school teaching

There is a certain amount of straightforward information that children need in order to provide material for their religious thought. The scope of this necessary factual information determines the contents of the academic curriculum. Summed up very briefly, all the knowledge that children should gain in the church school comes under three headings:

God is: growth in the knowledge of God.
The Church is: growth in the knowledge of the Church.
I am: growth in the knowledge of self.

Growth in the knowledge of God

With very young children the importance of telling Bible stories lies not so much in the actual plot of the story, but in the fact that the narrative conveys to the child the firm belief that *God is*. God is, and He acts in certain ways, and He has certain qualities; He shows Himself in the life of the people. In the Appendix to this book I have attempted to make a selection of stories arranged according to the developmental stages of childhood. The first ideas about God that a young child can grasp are those of His power, His love, and His concern for us.

As the child grows older, the idea of *God's law*, of the demands God lays upon us, has to be presented. The child's nascent moral sense has to be nurtured by exposing him to examples, stories and parables that are within his grasp and his capacity to recognize "right" and "wrong." Christian morality does not come naturally. It takes a certain kind of vision, a certain kind of imagination and thinking, for a child to recognize what is good and what is bad from the Christian point of view. I well remember my distress when I saw an eight-year-old boy who had just come out of church, where he had attended the Divine Liturgy, completely absorbed in burning out the eyes of a cycada and tearing off its wings. He did this without any sense of wrong-doing.

Along with the capacity to distinguish between "right" and "wrong" and the ability to recognize sin, we have to teach the child the importance of choice, the responsibility of choice, the actual inevitability of choice. The exacting demand of teaching children is that these concepts cannot be built up by moralizations, or verbalization of rules. They have to be made colorful and to come alive through stories, examples and real life situations. Then, when the image becomes alive for the child, its meaning can be summed up in a verbal formula, in a maxim or in a precept.

Only against the background of a child's growing comprehension of "right" and "wrong" and of the responsibility he undertakes for choices, can be born the experience of repentance, when he experiences grief at a broken relationship—with a parent, with a friend, or with God. The story of the Prodigal Son is the most direct and dramatic presentation of the theme of repentance. It can be understood in its simplest aspects by a seven-year-old and remains completely meaningful to the most spiritually mature adult. Lessons and narratives in class can help children realize the meaning of repentance. You can discuss with them the difference between the Prodigal Son's repentance and Adam's blaming of Eve. You can speak to twelve-year-olds about the difference between Peter's betrayal and that of Judas. Of course speaking about the meaning of repentance in class will be quite insufficient unless the children have the experience of going through the sacrament of Confession.

As church school students grow older, the whole realm of *meaning* becomes very important: the meaning of life, the meaning of suffering, the meaning of time, the meaning of salvation, the meaning of happiness. It is difficult to overestimate the power which indoctrination by all the media of their environment exerts on our young people, and the deep conflict which it arouses between a secularized world-view and that of Christianity. That young people do not ask any questions is usually not a good sign. It means simply that for them religion is enclosed in a very small and isolated compartment which has nothing to do with the rest of their life. The task of instructing our young adolescents in church school is precisely to bring out conflicts and questions, to examine their doubts and to provide them with a perspective against which life situations can be judged.

A good criterion of the success of a church school program is whether the graduating pupils are conscious of how little they know and whether they feel that they would like to know more. There is no moment when the process of acquiring knowledge about God and of God can stop. The best achievement of a church school program is simply to have the young people realize that this process is continuous and that it demands effort.

Growth in the knowledge of the Church

The life of the Church witnesses to the reality of God's presence in our life. The little child begins to be conscious of this through his physical senses when he sees, smells, touches the interior of the church building, the objects used, the lights, the priestly vestments, the physical elements of the sacraments. The very young child simply sees, tastes, touches, smells, and hears the things that make up the church. But what he thus perceives is just as true and valid as that which is perceived intellectually and spiritually by a mature person. Thus the first stage of church instruction for young children is to provide opportunities to learn all that pertains to the church through his senses. He should learn creatively by singing, moving, doing, even acting out procedures of behavior in church. The advantage of church school instruction at this early age is the fact that the *group* makes possible games, plays and crafts in a greater variety than at home. It is also possible within a church school to arrange for special visits to the church at a time when no service goes on. Then children can touch, look, investigate and ask questions on their own.

As the child grows older the main purpose of instruction about the Orthodox Church is to give them a better familiarity with the liturgical life of the church and a better understanding of it. This involves not only textbook information, but active participation of children in the services (something that a church school can plan better than an individual family): training altar boys, planning duties that can be carried out by the girls, organizing a junior choir that will sing some of the responses, taking part in processions and special ceremonies, reading in church. Ideally, most of the classroom instruction related to liturgical worship should be either a preparation for, or an explanation of, the actual experience of taking part in the service. I am afraid that much of our instruction in the past has been "putting the cart before the horse." Information and explanation become interesting and meaningful only when they are closely connected with the actual experience of the event or the action explained.

As our children reach adolescence, they have to come to terms with the concept of the Church as the Body, the incarnation of God in our life: What is the Church? What is my place in it? What does it mean for us? What is its place in the world?

It seems to me that it is impossible to gain a real understanding of these questions unless one has some knowledge of church history, of the problems the Church had to deal with in the past and of the thinking of some of its great saints. We all have had experience of youth groups floundering hopelessly in discussions that remained superficial because they were a mere exchange of ignorance. A good teenage curriculum in a church school should start with determining the greatest points of sensitivity and interest in the minds of young people and then provide the information that is relevant to these points of interest.

I knew a group of intelligent and rather sophisticated fourteen-year-old girls who, in reply to their teacher's questions during the first session, said they were not interested in discussing dating because they were too young and did not date. When the teacher asked them what they *would* want to discuss they came up quite unexpectedly with— abortion. For a few sessions rather unsatisfactory and vague discussions were held on this and other topics, and then the utterly frustrated teacher decided to go back to reading assignments in a church history textbook, so that the girls would get at least something out of the course. Perhaps, when the girls suggested the theme of abortion a better way to handle the situation would have been to assign some Bible and liturgical research: creation of man and woman according to the first chapters of Genesis, the role of the family and child-birth in God's promise to Abraham (Sarah laughed at the thought of having a child in her old age, the idea seemed so ridiculous; would abortion be justified?), the marriage rite, the Church's prayers for a woman who has had a miscarriage, and some articles in the more enlightened church magazines.

A church school curriculum for teenagers should also provide opportunity for *action* as a church group, projects for service that would help the young people to develop a sense of responsibility in church life. We want them to become adult lay people who are conscious that they are the Church, that they are parts of the Body which is the Church. How tiresomely often we hear: "Why doesn't the Church do this or that?" "Why is the Church thus and so?" whereas the real question is "Why don't *we* do this and that?" "Why are *we* thus and so?" Just as in any other form of learning, the principle of "learning by doing" applies in the church school and better than anything else it can help educate our young people in the experience of action and responsibility within the Church.

Growth in "knowledge of self"

Communicating information in a meaningful way is difficult enough, but there is another aspect of what takes place in a church school classroom situation—or rather should take place—that is far more difficult to define. For a child the experience of church school is *the* experience of taking part in church life. The small group in a church school class is in a sense a cell of the church Body. Within this cell an individual child discovers himself as a member of the Church. This, of course, involves the constant growth of the child's awareness of self. In this process the role of the teacher becomes even more important and more difficult than that of a "conveyer of information" and of "maintainer of discipline," although both these responsibilities are important in themselves. The "teacher-disciple" relationship, which is the ideal situation in a church school class, requires a teacher's real concern and effort to understand each child as a person. Every child behaves differently, every child in some way is a problem. Sometimes it is the child that causes no disciplinary problem at all that is the real problem child, because he cannot express himself. A good teacher must constantly try to understand "the reason why" behind a child's behavior, be always alert for symptoms, strive for new insights. He must never be satisfied with branding a child with a popular cliché, whether of the old-fashioned variety or in terms of the modern amateur psychologist. Children change as they grow, so that the effort to know them and understand them is a never-ending process. Throughout his contact with the children the teacher should maintain this effort; his attention and motivation must center on the child; he should always be eager and alert to gain a better insight into the personality of each pupil. A teacher of twelve-year-olds who was very successful in establishing this personal relationship with his students (in a small class) used the following technique: for a period of a few weeks he assigned individual research to the students and spent considerable time in individual conferences with each one of them. Their progress in self-realization and interest was quite marked.

Nurturing the child's awareness of himself as a "person under God" is one of the very important aims of Christian education, and the method of teaching in church school should be designed to further it.

In our work with pre-schoolers we can emphasize the five senses as gifts of God. Games and experiments involving the use of senses—tasting, seeing, listening, touching, smelling—should be part of some of the lessons. All stories told and all lessons taught should make an appeal to the child's perception by means of senses. Make them close their eyes to "feel" the darkness, make them move like the people or the animals mentioned in the story, make them listen to silence, make them imagine the taste of what you speak about, the coolness of water, the warmth of fire. Through stories told in such a manner we can encourage the very young child's wonder at the world surrounding him and at his own capacities and his own gifts. Repeating endlessly that "God made this..." and "God gave us that..." has not much meaning if it remains mere words and does not awaken the child's own wonder.

As the child grows older, more and more attention should be given to his creative involvement in the lesson. A lesson is good only if the pupil has put something of himself into it. All so-called activities, such as arts and crafts, poster-making and puppet shows, are useless and can be sheer waste of time unless the child expresses through them his own understanding, his own feelings and his own interpretation of the topic. Activities in class should serve as a means of helping the student "to make the material his own," to "assimilate" the contents of the lesson. This is not easy to achieve, but only insofar as the student puts something of himself into it does he make a drawing, a poster, or anything else of this kind truly creative.

Another aspect of the child's growing self-knowledge is

his ability to recognize his place among others. Of course he learns this all the time, at home, among his friends, in the street, or at school. But, in the experience of a child, the church school stands as an image of the Church, and thus recognizing his own place there and his relationship to others acquires a special meaning. One of the most important tasks of the teacher is to establish among the pupils an atmosphere of respect for each other's work, of interest in each other, of mutual recognition of achievements, of willingness to admit mistakes, of readiness to forgive, and of compassion. Each class has to become a "cell" within the Body of the Church. Only then can we speak of the church school as meaningful in Christian education.

In the case of older children it becomes more and more important to encourage them to express their thoughts on the subject that is being studied. It is not so much *what* is studied (because whatever we study will always be an infinitely small section of all we should know), but *how* it is studied that will help to develop the student's ability to think and encourage them to look for a deeper understanding. Very often youngsters come to class prepared to "swallow" what is being offered them, and the lesson does not trigger off any thinking process of their own. In a sense, a rebellious student who comes ready to challenge and criticize can be very helpful because it is indifference, apathy and lack of interest that are much harder to deal with. Personally I have often found it helpful at the beginning of a year's work with teenagers to have them answer anonymously in class some questionnaire with fairly provocative questions. This gives them a chance to express some of their latent doubts. Then I try to build a discussion or a lesson around the opinions expressed. It is very important to establish an atmosphere where students feel free to express their opinions and know that these opinions are treated with attention and respect. Other students should attempt to give answers, or disagree with an opinion expressed before the teacher expresses his own point of view. But he has to be ready to express it, to provide Christian insights into the question discussed and to give the factual information needed. This latter aspect is very important, for this is what makes the difference between true learning and a rather pointless exchange of casual and ignorant thinking, "pouring emptiness into a void" according to an old Russian proverb. The object of working with teenagers is to awaken their ability to question and wonder about life and to help them to discover where they can find answers.

The church school has done well in its instruction if the student comes to the point where he asks himself: Who am I? What do I believe? What does life mean? What does God and the Church mean in my life? Then he begins to see how some of these questions are answered in our Orthodox Christian faith.

What is a lesson?

Now at the end of more than fifty years of classroom teaching experience, I still face every class session with diffidence, a certain apprehension and a sense of challenge: maybe this time it will work out, a learning experience will take place, a thought will be born. However helpful a teacher's guide accompanying the textbook may be, a lesson has to be prepared and planned by the teacher himself. Besides the framework of the curriculum which determines the subject matter to be taught, besides considerations of liturgical calendar which determine some of the themes, there is a certain individual, personal planning through which I feel I have to go before every lesson.

1. *What* will I teach? What is important about it? What knowledge about God, about the Church or about human experience must it convey? How is the contents of the lesson relevant to the experience of the children? How is it relevant to the time of the year? I know that unless I am really penetrated by the importance of what I want to convey, unless it is colorful and alive for me, my lesson will not be interesting. This is when outside reading, any information I may have gleaned from actual happenings,

talks, lectures, sermons, becomes a kind of storehouse on which I have to draw.

2. *Whom* will I teach? I try to imagine the impact of my lesson on my pupils: Peter, David, Jessica, Susan and all the others. From my knowledge of them I try to guess what their reaction may be, what may interest particular ones among them, what are the difficulties I may expect, what would be the best way of dealing with them.

3. After thoroughly concentrating on these two aspects, I try to plan *how* I am going to teach my lesson. How will I introduce it to catch their interest and tie it in with what we have already done? How much time will I spend on the actual telling or conveying of new information? What questions will I ask? What will I expect the pupils to do themselves? What physical arrangements will be most helpful: standing, changing places, moving around, a game? These two pupils who keep talking to each other: shall I try to separate them, or shall I assign a task for them to do together? What aids will I need: paper, maps, blackboard, chalk, glue, scissors, or perhaps more sophisticated material: a tape recorder, or a projector?

However painstakingly I have prepared the lesson plan, it may work out differently. Some unexpected situation may arise and I must be flexible and omit a less important item, even if it was well planned, for the more important unexpected one. Probably other teachers prepare their lessons differently, but preparing a lesson must be a teacher's own creative act.

Criteria of church school instruction

In my opinion the instructional role of the church school has to be judged in the light of three criteria:

1. Does the contents of the lessons and the manner in which they are taught help the student to gain a knowledge about God, God's action in the world and his own relationship to God? I am quite consciously not so presump-

tuous as to say that the church school can give "knowledge of God"; but even "knowledge about God" is important in the process of gaining knowledge of God.

2. Does the church school help the student to feel part of the Church by leading him to experience and participate actively and understandingly in the liturgical services during the whole sequence of the liturgical year? Does it prepare the students to take an active part in the life of the parish?

3. Does the contents and manner of teaching help the child and the young person to become aware of himself as a person, under God and in relationship to other people?

It seems to me that all we do to improve our Christian educational programs and to train our teachers should keep these criteria in mind.

Church school and the liturgical year

The church school can help both the parish and the home to rediscover the meaning of the liturgical year, the meaning of the feasts celebrated by the Church, through which the content of the Christian faith is expressed. This task of the church school is at least as important as its instructional function.

"Celebrating" means embodying and implementing through action, in rites, songs and traditional usages, in food and in ceremonies, the meaning of some great event. In an earlier chapter I mentioned that celebrations and traditions connected with the feasts were born and developed under conditions of life and in a society very different from ours today. Many of them were connected with agricultural events, such as the blessing of fruit on the day of Transfiguration. This was a very meaningful rite that helped people realize the potential goodness and holiness of the whole world of nature and the joy of resurrection. It also included the natural joy of bringing to be blessed and made holy in church the first-fruits of the season, for which all had worked so hard. According to a pious custom no new fruit was eaten until it had been blessed on that day. But today for an average housekeeper the senses of "seasonal fruit" is practically lost. The "natural" aspect of the tradition is lost and it requires an effort of imagination to make it meaningful. New traditions and customs cannot be artificially established. Yet we can make an effort to discover how the important events remembered during the liturgical year can be reflected in the life of our society here and now. The church school is precisely that flexible unit within the parish where it is possible to try out new ways of remembering our feasts.

Here are some suggestions, beginning with the three major feasts at the beginning of the church school year.

On September 8 we remember the Birth of the Theotokos. Much is being said about the importance of establishing a close relationship between the church school, the home and the parents. This feast offers an excellent opportunity to celebrate, just as the school year begins, the idea of a Christian home. A gathering of the parents can be planned and announced on the Sunday preceeding the feast. It could be given the character of honoring parents, celebrating their role. The theme of the feast offers many ideas for this. On this day teachers could meet parents informally and discuss with them the children's needs and the work planned for the year. A certain parish priest had some misgiving about this kind of pre-celebration of a feast that comes on a weekday. To his astonishment he found that the Liturgy on the actual day of the feast was better attended after it had been "pre-celebrated" on the preceeding Sunday.

On September 14 we celebrate the Elevation of the Holy Cross. Usually this coincides with the beginning of church school. Children could be encouraged to make it a special "cross remembrance" day. As children register for school, the importance of wearing their baptismal crosses can be stressed. Crosses can be provided for those who do not have any. (Sometimes parents prefer for children not to wear constantly their original baptismal cross for fear of loss.) If the feast comes on a weekday, families can be encouraged to attend the evening service on the eve of the feast. In some churches the tradition of "elevating the cross" is observed during this evening service. It is very impressive.

On November 21 the Church celebrates the Entrance of the Theotokos into the Temple, a good occasion for celebrating the role of the church school in introducing the child into church life. By that time, church school is off to a good start and some preparations can be carried out. Children can pass on to parents invitations to attend the vigil service on the eve of the feast. There are many opportunities for the children's active participation during the service itself. In certain parts of Russia, I know, it was traditional for young girls and small children to stand with flowers and lighted candles in two rows in the middle of the church, symbolizing the friends of Mary who accompanied her to the Temple steps. The junior choir may be ready by this time to sing some of the simple responses, and some of the older children can prepare to read the "Paremia," or Old Testament readings. There is no doubt that the active participation of their children will encourage many of the parents to attend the service too.

The period of Advent begins six days before the feast of the Entrance of the Theotokos into the Temple. Unless the church school finds some way to bring it to the children's attention, there is a good chance that it will remain unnoticed and unobserved. Teachers must remember that they cannot attempt to impose fasting rules on children, since the home diet rules are established by the parents. Yet somehow the idea of a gradual approach to the coming feast, the expectation of it, the preparation for it, should be reflected in the church school program. There is a non-Orthodox tradition (German, I believe) of hanging up a wreath of pine boughs with candles, their number corresponding to the number of weeks before Christmas. The first candle is lit on the first week of Advent and every Sunday an additional candle is lighted. I think this could easily be adapted for church school use. Another tradition is to set up a manger scene, gradually adding all the figures during the Advent season, with the figure of the Christ Child placed on the eve of the feast.

Another good Advent theme is one of gifts, and the children can become involved in preparing them for some special project. St. Nicholas Day on December 6 is a good opportunity to offer gifts in a home for the aged or in a children's hospital. Rehearsals for carol singing can be meaningful too, as can the preparation of some kind of Christmas program. A special day can be set aside for children to go to Confession and to receive Holy Communion.

The question of special Christmas programs is more debatable. Children's Christmas vacations seem to be crowded with so many events and celebrations that teachers wonder whether another fairly elaborate one, demanding rehearsals and a lot of additional work for teachers and parents, is really necessary. Sometimes so much emphasis is laid on ethnic elements, on dances, songs and acting, that the program in no way serves to bring the children any closer to an understanding of the meaning of the Lord's Nativity. On the other hand it is very important that a real "fun-time" should be part of the children's experience of celebrating a church feast.

I can see two approaches to a special Christmas program. In a large school that has a large hall with a stage, many teachers and pupils, and parents willing to help, it may be a good idea to have a good and aesthetically satisfying program or pageant interpreting the meaning of Christ's Nativity in the language of art. I have seen some beautiful programs, which were meaningful both for the children taking part in them and for the audiences. In smaller schools a special Christmas program may be a good opportunity for establishing a closer rapport with the home—between parents, teachers and children. If the teaching has been creative and has involved work done by the students themselves, it is neither difficult nor time-consuming for each class to show something of what they have done in graphic or dramatic form: singing games by the pre-schoolers, puppet shows, simple dramatizations by primary children, art exhibits or slide and movie shows by the seniors. Parents are usually willing to work on refreshments, small gifts can be exchanged and the whole party becomes a kind of family reunion.

The feast of Epiphany on January 6 provides an opportunity for preparing the children to receive holy water and for the blessing of homes. This is still one of the more faithfully observed feasts, and parents can be encouraged to have their children released from public school to attend the Divine Liturgy. In one parish the priest moved the time for the blessing of the water to the eve of the feast, so that high school students could attend it after school, and arranged for a lot of participation by the students. In another church school, children were actively enlisted to prepare containers for holy water.

The Meeting of the Lord, on February 14, seems a good opportunity to honor the aged. It can be made a kind of church "grandparents' day." Since the loneliness and prolonged helplessness of the very aged is a marked trait in our society today, this feast gives an opportunity for drawing our own attention and that of the children to what can be done.

With the beginning of Great Lent we are entering the most meaningful time of the church school year. Most textbooks published by the Orthodox Christian Education Commission contain whole units on the pre-lenten period, Great Lent and Pascha. I shall not attempt to outline these programs here, for they are easily available. It has also become traditional to hold young people's retreats during Great Lent and for children to go to Confession and receive Holy Communion. It should be a real cause for concern how superficially and mechanically many church schools "organize" the children's Confession and Communion, so that the whole experience becomes an exercise in a legalistic approach to "fulfilling one's yearly church duty." A year or two ago, however, I was privileged to take part in a rather unusual way to have church school children come to Confession and Communion during Great Lent. A letter was sent out to all parents some two weeks before the date set. Classes met on Friday afternoon and all the teachers tried to prepare their children for a better understanding of Confession and Communion. After church school a brief service of Vespers was held. The priest spoke to the children about the meaning of Confession. He addressed himself mainly to the older children, speaking of their difficulties and doubts in regard to Confession. An example he gave seems to have made a powerful impression on them:

> Why do we have to *tell* the priest about our sins? If we are sorry and tell God, is it not enough? Putting something in words, telling about it to someone, has a special importance. When I was a small boy I used to play every afternoon with my best friend, and our favorite game was setting up our army of toy tin soldiers. I was especially proud of a little machine gun that someone had given me and I even marked it a special way. Then one day the machine gun disappeared. What was worse, I discovered that my friend had taken it. Because of the little mark I had made, there was no doubt in my mind. I said nothing and my friend said nothing, but our happy little world lay in ruins. I *knew* that he took it, and *he knew that I knew* that he took it, and *I knew that he knew that I knew*. We could not face each other, we could not play together. Then, in a day or two he came up to me and said: "I am sorry. I took your gun. Forgive me." "O, forget about it," I answered. "What do I care!" Suddenly all the world around us was bright and happy again. Everything was so good that it felt like Easter.

The children I spoke to after the service mentioned this story as the part of the sermon that impressed them most. When the service was over the priest heard confessions of children, parents and teachers.

All the children were in some way actively involved in the Liturgy on Saturday morning. The older girls baked the prosfora. All the children prepared lists of names of people for whom they wanted to pray. The Proskomedia was performed in the middle of the church, and as the priest took up the bread and cut out the particles, each child read aloud the names of the people on his list, the friends whom he wished to remember during the Divine Liturgy. As many children as possible read, sang and served as altar boys. Everyone partook of Holy Communion and then breakfast was served. The school was a small one, but I believe that in larger schools it would still be possible to make this kind of experience available, preferably going by groups of families rather than by grades.

Holy Week and Easter services are usually well attended by Orthodox families. The function of the church school is mainly to prepare the children for these days in advance, making sure that they know and understand their meaning. It is a good idea to make available small, inexpensive booklets that will help the children to follow the services, such as the text of the twelve Gospel readings for the evening of Holy Thursday.

Most church schools close around Pentecost. To hold the school closing exercises on Pentecost Sunday is not convenient because of the great length of the service, but the inner link between the feast and the teaching task of the Church should be emphasized and maintained. The school, both students and teachers, can be mentioned and honored in the sermon on Pentecost Sunday. In some churches it is traditional for the faithful to hold flowers during this service, and I have known parishes where little bouquets of flowers were prepared by the children and distributed by them to all the people entering the church.

These are just a few random suggestions on how the liturgical calendar can be reflected in the life of the church school. Many other ideas and suggestions could be developed. I am sure that such an approach would be helpful to the children, making them realize more vividly their membership in the Church. It also would be a good way to revitalize the meaning of feasts in our parishes. The underlying principle is that the church school carries out its functions only if it introduces the child to the experience of living in the Church.

CHAPTER V

The Teacher

The parish priest can approach the religious education of his adult parishioners in several ways: he has a captive audience when he preaches the Sunday sermon; he comes into a more intimate spiritual contact with them through general and individual confession; the whole structure of parish life, including the liturgical services and the common work, involves the participation of adult members of the parish. But all these approaches are, in a way, above the heads of our children; and the teaching mission carried on by the church school, under the guidance of the priest, consists precisely in introducing the younger generation into the fulness of the life of the Church. In this mission good lay teachers, who can translate their own authentic experience of church life into the language of the children's experience, are the most crucial link. No books, however good, no programs, however well prepared, will replace the personal influence of the teacher. Whatever methods he uses, the teacher will leave his personal imprint on the contents he presents in class. An inspired and open-minded teacher will use the most old-fashioned and formal textbooks in a creative way. The most progressive manual will be taught mechanically by a legalistic and narrow-minded instructor.

Finding good teachers for the church school is one of the most difficult and responsible tasks of the parish priest.

Ideally a church school teacher should have three qualifications:

1. He must have an authentic experience of participating in church life, on however modest a scale. In other words, his Orthodox faith, however incomplete, must be his own sincere faith.

2. He must have a capacity, perhaps only a potential one, for communicating with children.

3. He must have the capacity to grow and develop his gifts.

Obviously some candidates will have one or the other of these qualities more strongly developed, but all three are equally important. Many lay people who sincerely would like to serve the Church hesitate to assume the duty of teaching our Orthodox Christian faith to our children because they feel they are not qualified to do so. I shall try to present in this chapter some of my thoughts on what it takes to be a teacher, based on my own long experience in church school work.

The teacher as a person

In order to face the many deflating and ego-destroying experiences involved in teaching children, a teacher must have faith in himself, faith in his own vocation. Curiously enough, this faith in oneself involves a deep sense of humility. Only humility gives you a sense of inner security. You do not overestimate your own capacities, you accept the fact that you are no genius. You find it natural that not all pupils find you likeable, that not all of them are interested in your best-prepared lesson. Humility protects you from getting unduly upset by the occasional failure of your teaching: "Who am I to be successful? I just have to try again and again." And in carrying out the teacher's responsibility of leadership and class discipline, humility saves your actions (or lack of action) from being inspired by a frustrated and insecure ego.

A teacher must be conscious of the limitations of his contacts with the child in class. He cannot "play psychiatrist," for he has neither the qualifications nor the knowledge of the child's background that are necessary for this. The contacts he has with the child in church school and in related activities are only a part of the child's total life. He has to deal with the child within this small section of the child's experience, using his best insights to understand the meaning of and reasons for the child's behavior (shyness or boysterousness, disinterest or lack of cooperation), trying to discover approaches that work. But he must realize the limitations of his scope. In other words, a teacher cannot "play God." Yet from our own childhood memories we know how some occasional word or action of a teacher, some minor incident, sometimes leaves an impression that lasts for years.

A teacher has to be conscious of his personal talents and of his personal limitations. Some are natural storytellers and can always hold a class's attention by this means; others, on the contrary, are best at drawing out the children's reactions and quietly observing them. Some have a special gift for making things clear, others are artistic or musical. A teacher should have a good idea of his own capacities and how they can be used.

Everyone would agree that the capacity to love children is the most important trait to be looked for in teachers. It is important, however, to realize just what we mean by love. It certainly does not mean finding them "cute," or "adoring the little angels." Neither does it mean liking them all equally, for certainly one child can be more likeable than another. Again I have to go back to the definition of love given in I Corinthians: "patient and kind, not jealous or boastful, not arrogant or rude, not insisting on its own way, not irritable or resentful, not rejoicing at wrong, but rejoicing at right, bearing all things, believing all things, hoping all things." I have often tried to apply these standards to the many situations that arise in classroom. Rejoicing when an arrogant and unpleasant pupil proves to be right? Hoping that the most hopeless clown in your class will be touched by the grace of the Holy Spirit? Not being arrogant in the way you present your lesson? Respecting each child and treating him with courtesy? The fact of the matter is that this kind of love matters most *for the teacher*, enriches the life of the teacher, changes him into something different from "a noisy gong or a clanging cymbal." Seeing children with the eyes of love nurtures the growth of the teacher as a person.

Another very important trait of the teacher's "self" is an authentic interest in life, or at least in several aspects of life, an attitude of curiosity to the many things that take place or have taken place in the world. A person completely and exclusively immersed in parish life does not make for a good teacher. In a sense such an attitude means that our Christian faith has nothing to do with life in general, with all of life. Especially through late childhood and adolescence, children tend to respect the knowledgeability of professionally qualified people, whether from the field of science, or art, or technology, or sports or anything else. Even an adult person's special hobby or interest can help to overcome the secularistic split between formal religion and the rest of life. This is the great advantage of having lay teachers. Youngsters will take for granted that it is the priest's business to believe in God, to believe in the Church. But to have a lay business man, or an engineer or an artist profess his faith may outweigh in importance that person's insufficient theological training (if only he is not religiously arrogant!).

I should mention here, as a kind of summary for what has been said above, that it is the teacher's image as a person, the example of his "self," that will finally determine his influence on his pupils. If his faith, however small, is sincere and authentic, if he is religiously a "growing" person, not a stagnating one, if he is open-minded and interested, humble (which in practice often means having a sense of humor), loving and, not least of all, conscientious, he has the makings of a good teacher.

Communicating with children

Not everyone has this inborn gift, but without it it is very difficult to become a good teacher. Yet it is possible to develop and increase this ability. First of all, the ability to communicate with children involves the ability to see them as they are, to recognize the level at which we can communicate with them. If we read the Gospel accounts from this point of view, we will see that Jesus Christ did this constantly in establishing contact with the people whom He taught or to whose needs He ministered. I think it would be a very helpful exercise or test, one that might become a part of a teacher training program, to have an adult spend an hour alone with a child or a small group of children, at play or at work, not trying to teach them anything, but just observing them, communicating with them, trying to discover how much he can find out about this particular child or children, about their ideas, their tastes, their feelings.

When actually teaching a class, notes should be kept on individual children, on their reactions, their behavior, their participation. Such notes will help the teacher to establish a bridge of communication with each child. Too often one has a tendency to be carried away by the contents of the lesson, by the desire to convey information. The student who helps in this process gets attention, the ones that do not get involved are disregarded. Yet the shy, withdrawn child, the noisy "attention-getter," the child absorbed in something of his own need much more badly the teacher's attention and some bridge of communication with the teacher. Regular notes on children do help, for we tend to forget just what took place a week ago. If one had to criticize a child, or reprove or discipline him, it is important to look out for an occasion to show appreciation. If a very shy child makes a positive contribution, it may be a good idea to refer to it several times in the course of the work to show its value, instead of simply complementing him. Some individual children are extremely hard to integrate into group work and become very disruptive. It may help to give them individual assignments that keep them busy on their own and yet are part of the total work.

Whatever the teacher does, whatever tricks of the trade he uses to involve his students in the process of learning, the effort to know children, to draw close to them, reducing one's own self-consciousness to the point of becoming child-conscious, is a very important part of the teacher's spiritual growth.

Leading and working with a group

The ability to communicate with individual children is the basis of the teacher's work, but more than this is involved in a classroom situation. The discipline of formal classroom instruction, with its emphasis on the pupil's silence and quiet behavior during the presentation of a lesson, has lost favor. The emphasis now is on involving the pupils' *creative* participation in the learning process, on "learning by doing," on the "open classroom." This type of teaching is much more demanding for the teacher and can easily degenerate into a pretty chaotic situation, leading to the general confusion of the pupils, the teacher and the parents. For example, a gifted teacher I knew came insufficiently prepared to teach a lesson in a class that was not yet used to independent work and was divided into small cliques. Spontaneously she decided to replace the lesson by an informal game, hoping it would establish better communication among the children. The game was taken up enthusiastically by one clique, but the other two boys wandered away, refusing to take part. Thus the lesson was not given, the game did not serve its purpose, and the parents, who had driven long distances to bring children to church school, watched the whole procedure dispiritedly, feeling it was a loss of the children's, the teacher's and their own time.

Working with a group creatively takes a lot of planning and preparation. First of all the objective, the goal of each lesson period, must be perfectly clear to the teacher: We shall try to get from this point, where we are now, to that point, which we have not yet reached. For example, a sixth grade studying the sacraments took up the sacrament of Baptism last time; the students brought their baptismal certificates; they discussed the meaning of membership in the Church. The purpose of this lesson is to gain a better understanding of the symbolism of the baptismal rites. In the introduction the teacher will have to remind the class of what was said last time. In order to provide flexible and varied ways of reaching the objective, he can then suggest that each student write up two or three questions that they would like to have answered in order to better understand what happens during Baptism. After collecting the questions, the class can be divided into several teams in order to do research work to find the answers. One team may look up the rite in the service book; another team may look up references to Baptism in the New Testament; a third may look up the appropriate chapter on Baptism in the church history textbook; another team may plan a poster on the elements used in Baptism and their symbolic meaning. This approach means that the teacher must have all the resource materials ready and at his finger tips: the service book, copies of the New Testament with lists of references to be looked up, a textbook on church history, materials for posters. If time permits the teams can report on their work at the end of the class period, or else the presentation of reports can be put off to the next class period. Even in a well-organized class, with clear instructions provided, there will still be movement, action, and talking. Students will take time to settle down to their work; there will be some arguments, some misunderstandings. The teacher has to keep a flexible kind of order and exercise some authority to maintain a working atmosphere.

The children have to be trained for this type of work by a new kind of discipline, a discipline of respect for each other's work. Creating an environment of creativity and freedom in class does not mean relinquishing authority. Authority and discipline in class must be based on a hierarchy of values. It is not a matter of the teacher's personal prestige, of his having to "save face," or of his authority being undermined by a sarcastic or discourteous remark. But the teacher cannot renounce his responsibility for leadership and authority; he must have a sense of the value of what is being done by the group. One student's misbehavior or clowning should not disrupt the work of the whole group, and I believe that a teacher should deal with such a situation quite firmly, making the child leave the room if necessary. It is important to create among the children a respect for the work they are doing. This does not mean, though, that the difficult student should not be an object of special concern and personal attention. Tasks should be found for him that will help him to get involved in the common work. Neither does it mean that there should not be some leniency and flexibility in letting the whole group relax, enjoy a joke or take a little time before they settle down to work.

How much should a teacher know?

It is almost impossible to set standards for the academic qualifications of church school teachers. The decisive factor is the teacher's willingness to *learn*. Every teacher, without exception, must try to learn at least a little more than is contained in the textbook he uses. For this, the curriculum and the teacher's guides published by the Orthodox Christian Education Commission are extremely helpful. When teacher training courses are planned or reading programs prepared, we should aim at least at a basic, well-rounded knowledge of what our Orthodox Christian faith means. A teacher should have a pretty thorough knowledge of the New Testament, including the Acts and the Epistles, so that the figures of the New Testament are really alive for him. He should have a good general idea of the meaning of the Old Testament, especially those aspects of it that foreshadow our Christian faith. As far as the liturgical life of the Church is concerned, he must know and understand at least the sacraments of the Church and those forms of liturgical worship that are practiced in his parish. He should know something of doctrine, at least within the scope of the Nicene Creed. He should also know something about the past of our Church and about some of the saints.

Much more difficult to define is the kind of Orthodox frame of mind that is the natural heritage of Christians who grow up in the church tradition and are nurtured by it. We live at a time of cultural changes. We are taking part in the process of creating an Orthodox way of life, an Orthodox tradition, in a society that did not know Orthodoxy, and at a time when this society is going through tremendous moral and spiritual upheavals. In this situation we are constantly faced by choices and decisions: How does the Orthodox attitude to death fit in with the modern American funeral home? How does the Orthodox experience of the sacrament of Healing relate to the "spiritual healing" advocated by many today? What is our Orthodox taste in the matter of improvised public prayers? This entire realm of what I would call "Orthodox taste" is extremely important in the way it affects the personality and the behavior of our teachers. I can think of no better guideline for this difficult task than the definition of the essence of Orthodoxy given by Berdyaev: "Fulfilment of freedom in and through the fulfilment of catholicity ['sobornost']."*

Teacher training

It is not within the scope of this book to speak in detail of teacher training programs. In order to be helpful, a full manual should be written on the subject. I do wish, however, to point out certain principles on which such programs should be based.

Teacher training has to be a continuous process. It cannot be a one-shot affair. During the long years of my work in the Orthodox Christian Education Commission I was often invited to speak to teachers at either parish or pan-Orthodox conferences. The audiences were usually re-

---

*I heard this definition given by Berdyaev in reply to a question by the well-known Baptist preacher Sherwood Eddy, during a conversation in which I acted as interpreter.

sponsive, and I met with sincere enthusiasm when I tried to present the goals of our work, the meaning of Christian education, or to describe the spiritual needs of childhood. In so many cases, however, it was frustrating to realize that this experience would not really help those attending to become better teachers. It might give them a moment of inspiration; some might be helped to catch a vision of what Orthodox Christian education should be; but the experience did not relate to their ability to implement their vision, to their ability to teach. The teachers' workshops that have been organized in later years by my successors have tried to teach actual teaching skills—the use of arts and crafts, for instance—with the active participation of teachers in carrying out the work. But the organizers of these workshops also have mentioned a sense of frustration because many of the participants had no real understanding of the basic goals of Christian education, of the "reason why" behind the activities suggested. The most beneficial result of all these efforts has been their overall effect on those laymen and laywomen whom you find coming again and again to whatever conference or workshop or course is being offered. Gradually a part of our laity, some of our "people of the Church," have been enlightened by the spirit of the Church's mission to the children and the young. Those of us who are old enough to remember the almost total absence of this consciousness in the traditionally Orthodox "old countries" can realize that the vocation of Christian education may be the special challenge, the special responsibility, the special grace of the Orthodox in America.

I believe that in planning teacher-training programs a certain wholeness should be always kept in mind. If the emphasis is on techniques and skills, there should at least be a strong presentation of the meanings which are conveyed through these techniques. If the emphasis is on conveying knowledge about our Christian faith—Bible, liturgics, doctrine, church history—there should be very practical illustrations of how this knowledge is incorporated into our curriculum at its different levels. If the basic principles of Orthodox Christian education are the program's theme—

the role of the church school, the role of the family, participation of children in liturgical life, etc.—then the participants should be drawn into the practical work of planning the implementation of these principles into the curriculum and methods of teaching. In other words, each unit of a teacher-training program, whatever its particular theme, should keep in mind the basic questions: What do we teach? Why do we teach? Whom do we teach? How shall we teach?

Teacher training has taken many forms. The various yearly conferences—one-day or two-day or three-day ones—have the advantage of more time at one occasion. They also provide opportunity for the experience of common liturgical life. But they take considerable preparatory work that can not be replaced by wishful thinking. At a conference of this type that I attended once, planned for 50 people, there was a 50% change of audience for each of the three lectures; of those registered only 10% attended the Liturgy; Vespers was cancelled; and there were no exhibits or workshops. However sincere the interest of those attending, the usefulness of such a conference is extremely limited, especially if there is no follow-up.

Another useful form of teacher training is the weekly course that runs for several weeks. This is not only a form of teacher training but also serves as adult education. It depends, of course, on the availability of good lecturers and their ability to speak in a way that relates to the "felt needs" of the audience. Whatever themes of doctrine, liturgics, Bible study, church history, etc. are presented, it is their meaning for the individual life needs of the listeners that will make them interesting.

I have already mentioned workshops carried out with the specific goal of teaching participants certain teaching skills: the use of music, arts and crafts, leading discussions, etc. But one further form of teacher training, modest and yet very useful, should be mentioned: regular meetings of teachers within the same church school, or even within the same department of the church school, preferably of those whose pupils are roughly of the same age. Sharing problems, planning the curriculum and special events, evaluating results, occasionally observing each other's work can be helpful. If it is possible to enrich such meetings with occasional book reports given by the members of the group, the entire experience becomes extremely valuable.

A church school teacher's vocation

I would like to finish this chapter and this book by speaking about the church school teacher's vocation. But first, what does "vocation" mean? In his talk with Motovilov, Saint Seraphim of Sarov spoke of the purpose of human life. He said that it consists in "acquiring the grace of the Spirit of God by those means that you find most advantageous." He explained that the meaning of any action, or any way of life, is not in what you actually do, but in the measure in which your work or your action fills you with the Spirit of God. Some people, he said, may find themselves enriched by this Grace when they actively help the poor, others when they live in lonely meditation, still others through some creative activity. The important thing is whether your activity brings into your heart the inspiration of divine Grace. Then your work, whether it be gardening or composing or fasting or helping others, will become your real vocation.

When being with children, loving children, participating in their growth, is *for you* a channel of Grace, when you feel that your own personality becomes more and more real as you communicate with children, then, I believe, you have a teacher's vocation, then the Lord's words about children— "of such is the Kingdom of Heaven"—have a special, personal meaning for you.

No teacher will ever feel that it is the children's moral goodness that inspired the words of Jesus. It always seemed to me that quite other qualities make up this special "charisma" of childhood. I think, first of all, of children's realism and simplicity in matters of religion. They have none of the adults' dualism. A young child's religious life is

whole: God, Heaven, angels are on the same level of matter-
of-factness as a toy, a playmate, a cat. The child in church
is the same child as on the playground (to our considerable
distress sometimes). There is a freshness of perception in
children. The colors of everything are so bright, the smells
so keen. Children do not stagnate; they grow, and the process
of growth *is* the essence of religious life. Everything in a
child is in a state of change, and in this change there is
always hope. A hurt or a disappointment quickly becomes a
thing of the past, and therein lies the child's true capacity
to forgive, when forgiving means forgetting. Children are
often arrogant and boastful, but this boasting is superficial
because fundamentally they *know* that they know very little,
that they cannot do much, that they are weak; and thus
childhood breathes an air of humility. Whatever are the
traits of children that make the Kingdom of Heaven theirs,
as long as we adults keep in touch with this world of childhood, we manage to "keep our foot in the door." Something
of this special grace of childhood rubs off on us.

There is one more way in which teaching religion to
our children influences us. In religious education we deal
with the very core of human personality, the very core of
life. Religious education means nurturing the growing human
soul in its relationship to God and to follow human beings.
In dealing with these essentials, we must become penetrated
by them ourselves. We must possess the religious knowledge we teach, and we must be possessed by the contents
of this knowledge. You cannot teach children the story of the
Resurrection unless you are filled with its meaning, unless
the religious truth of this fact has become part of you.
Unless in your mind and heart you are there with Mary of
Magdala, with John and Peter, unless you have experienced the breathless haste of Peter, unless you have said
with Mary "Master . . ." you cannot convey to children the
meaning of the Easter story. If you are a Christian educator,
you constantly must be penetrated with the great facts of
Christianity.

We can go through life as if the world were not created
by God, as if Christ were not born, as if He did not die and

did not rise from the dead. Our natures are lazy and un-imaginative. Then, suddenly, we have to teach all this. We become the vehicles through which these events make their impact on a child's growing mind. It is indeed a stimulating experience to become a wire through which passes this power-ful electric current. Once you have experienced this, you have found a real vocation and it holds you.

Appendix

The Appendix is by no means a curriculum. It is an attempt to organize our thinking on the basis of what we believe about Orthodox Christian education, and in a way that will help the work of preparing a curriculum. My hope is that it may prove useful to curriculum committees, priests, church school supervisors, and teachers. They should approach these guidelines critically, discarding some ideas and adding new ones. On the basis of the text they can try to plan a curriculum that will answer the needs of their parish.

The guidelines are presented in the form of four columns. The first column is based on what leading religious educators today define as the "Developmental stage" of each age group. For the formulation of the definitions it contains I am particularly indebted to the book *Readiness for Religion,* by Ronald Goldman. The second column lists "Concepts that can be taught" at each stage of development, the third one the "Curriculum contents" through which such concepts can be presented and the fourth one contains some comments on the methods of presenting these contents to that particular age group.

I have chosen ten basic areas of life experience and knowledge under which I grouped the contents in each column:

1. Family
2. Self

3. Community
4. Church
5. World
6. God
7. Prayer
8. Symbolism
9. Moralism
10. Historical Consciousness

These guidelines are not based on any particular set of books, nor on any particular existing curriculum, though my approach is definitely influenced by the work of the Orthodox Christian Education Commission. The same kind of thinking that went into the preparation of OCEC textbooks is reflected in the present guidelines.

Early childhood: age 5, 6 and 7

Developmental stage

1. Family: The child is still strongly family-centered and needs constantly to refer to the security of the family environment, but the sense of parental omnipotence begins to be eroded. Since the large family clan is not much present in modern American life, the child's experience outside the home is mainly reduced to that of contemporaries in school and to the world of TV.

2. Self: Egocentric, unable to take the viewpoint of another person. Can understand concrete operations but is unable to cope with problems related to measurement and time causality. Short attention span. Difficulties in remaining motionless for any length of time. Excellent memory for simple short words accompanied by gesture and/or melody.

Concepts that can be taught

Parents are interested in what we do in church school. The church school teacher is interested in what we do at home. Parents take part in church school.

Caring for others: pets, people. Beginning to be able to see how another person feels. We are sorry when someone is hurt. We enjoy taking part in a singing game, or a round game with simple rules.

Contents of curriculum

Bible stories with emphasis on family: How God saved Noah's family and animal families; God's promise to Abraham; baby Moses; the nativity of Christ. The birth of Mary. Her presentation in the Temple. Stories of major feasts related to family traditions.

Bible stories: Abraham and Lot make up a quarrel; Balaam's ass (learning from animals); the little boy who gave Jesus his bread and fish; the Good Samaritan. Real-life stories of children helping others and taking care of pets or plants. Stories of animals. Stories and games that help children to use their senses.

Teaching methods

Parents should be kept in close touch with what the teacher is trying to do in class. A child should have a leaflet to take home and some of his work to show to parents after every lesson. Parents should be invited for observation and individual conferences with teachers. Children should be encouraged to share in class anything of interest that they bring from home ("show and tell").

Stories told should appeal to the five senses and involve children's active participation. Children can act out stories and illustrate them in various ways. Games allowing expression of concepts by gesture and action. Lesson divided into several short periods involving change of place and movement and type of attention.

133

Early childhood: age 5, 6 and 7

Developmental stage	Concepts that can be taught	Contents of curriculum	Teaching methods
3. Community: Experienced mainly through school and play companions of the same age.	We play and work together in church school.	**Bible stories:** How the First Church was built (story of the Tabernacles); Jesus and the children; how Jesus gave Holy Communion to His friends. Story of how the parish church was built.	Friendly, relaxed atmosphere established in the church school class is more important than the information conveyed. Calm and sympathetic attention to the individual child within the framework of the established order.
4. Church: Understood strictly as the church building.	This is our church. What we do and see in church. There are special days like Christmas and Easter that are special in church and at home.	The shape of the church building. The things we see in church. The priest and his helpers. What do we see and hear in church on Sundays?	All the information should be built around what the children perceive by their senses. Visit arranged to the church when there are no services going on when the children can touch and examine all they see. Training in the physical aspects of church behavior: sign of the cross, kneeling, kissing an icon, putting up a candle, approaching Holy Communion.

134

5. World: Inability to categorize and separate reality from fantasy. Human characteristics and powers often given to inanimate objects. Answers to many questions sought, but every answer makes sense and is accepted.

Everything God made is good. There are some bad things in the world. We try to help God by taking care of things.

Bible stories: Creation of the world (visible and invisible); the Fall; verses from Psalm 104.

Using audio-visual aids and simple experiments, children can be helped to perceive the wonder of the God-created world: plants growing, life of animals. Collecting leaves, flowers, rocks. Posters made of children's illustrations to Psalm 104. Children telling in class about their pets and about people they know who help God to take care of the world: the doctor, the nurse, the ranger, etc.

6. God: God is willingly recognized as "the one who made everything" when this is stated by adults. Jesus Christ is recognized as someone who was very good and helped people.

God made the world. God cares for us. God helps us and gives us things. God wants us to be good and happy. Jesus helps people. God loves us even when we have been bad.

Sign of the cross. "In the name of the Father and of the Son and of the Holy Spirit." Bible stories preparing for the concept of the Holy Trinity: Creation (Gen. 1: God, the Word of God, the Spirit of God); icon of the visit of the Three Angels; God speaks to Moses on the mountain. New Testament: Nativity, Epiphany, Jesus and the children, calming the tempest, healing the paralytic, Jesus and Zacchaeus, entry to Jerusalem, Last Supper, Crucifixion, Resurrection, Ascension, Pentecost.

Unless children ask specific questions there does not seem any need to emphasize the doctrinal ideas contained in the Bible stories presented. The purpose of telling them is to accumulate impressions and preliminary ideas of what God does. These will be interpreted later.

Early childhood: age 5, 6 and 7

Developmental stage	Concepts that can be taught	Contents of curriculum	Teaching methods
7. Prayer: On one hand prayers and church rites are perceived as obligations imposed by parents. On the other hand there is willing acceptance of the automatic and magical validity of prayer.	When we pray, we speak to God. We ask Him to help us and others. We thank Him.	Short prayer sentences that enable the children to join in liturgical worship: "In the name of the Father and of the Son and of the Holy Spirit," "Lord, have mercy," "Glory to Thee, O God," "Alleluia," "Grant it, O Lord," and others. Gradual memorization of the Lord's Prayer. Stories from lives of saints and from life today about how people pray to God.	Short prayers can be memorized by singing or reciting them in class. Children can be encouraged to make up simple prayers and "litanies" of their own, asking God for what they need and thanking Him. Preparing lists of names of family and friends to be remembered in individual prayer or during Divine Liturgy.
8. Symbolism: The symbolism of things is readily acceptable, i.e. a stick is a gun, etc. But the symbolic meaning of stories is often interpreted quite irrelevantly.	The things we see and do in church mean something special.	Things used symbolically in church: a lighted candle is a prayer, incense is our praise of God, the cross on the church building shows that it is God's house, priestly vestments mean a special gift of God and so on. Symbolism of bread and wine, of oil and water.	Instruction should be built around the physical perception of the symbolic object. See suggestions under 4, above.

136

9. Moralism: Evil is identified with the material harm done, with parental or social disapproval, with the severity of the punishment. Any injustice or hurt to oneself is strongly felt, but there is little perception of hurting others or of being unjust to them. Good is identified with approval.

Some people are very good: they help others, they love others, they forgive when they are hurt. We can choose between doing "bad" or doing "good." God wants us to be good. We are sorry when we do something bad or hurt someone. When we are sorry for doing something bad, God always forgives us.

O.T. Bible stories: Origin of evil; fall of the proud angel; Adam and Eve in the Garden; their disobedience; Cain and Abel; David and Goliath. N.T. Bible stories: the Prodigal Son; forgiving others as God forgives us (Matt. 18:23-35); passages from the Sermon on the Mount (Matt. 5:23-25; 6:2-4; 7:1-5). Incidents from lives of saints. Modern-life stories illustrating moral problems within a child's experience of life.

The purpose of the stories selected is to enrich the child's concept of what is "good" and what is "bad," though it is still too early to attempt to analyze why an action is good or bad. One should beware of carrying on discussions when children will repeat opinions expressed by the adults in their environment without any real understanding of the moral values involved. The general atmosphere created in the classroom by the teacher (i.e. friendliness, interest in each child's achievement, compassion and sympathy, maintenance of simple discipline such as waiting for one's turn and keeping the rules of games and work, willingness to help each other) is more important than the stories told.

10. Historical consciousness: Sense of time limited to "once upon a time"... The story is unfolded in imagination. It is the time of the marvelous. There is no sense of chronology, nor of chronological sequence of events, no sense of historical development.

Towards the end of this age period the children are ready for the basic concept that some of the Bible stories took place before Jesus Christ was born, others are about Jesus Christ and that stories from the lives of saints are about how people lived after Jesus Christ went back to heaven.

No attempt is made to present a Biblical chronology of events, except for a gradual distinction between Old Testament and New Testament events. The major events of the life of Jesus Christ will gradually fall into a certain sequence, but this need not be emphasized.

Middle childhood: age 8, 9 and 10

Developmental stage

1. Family: Parents are somewhat reduced in stature, but there is still a great need for the security of the family structure and parental love and authority. Children tend to accept their parents as they are, fairly uncritically. Sibling conflicts and competition for attention quite strong.

2. Self: The children's thinking has progressed to the ability to draw conclusions from the concrete to the general, but they are not capable of abstract thinking. "Cause and effect" perception is well developed with a tendency to a primitive kind of rationalism. Strong conscious sensitivity to personal relations of the "I and you" type, a desire to make friends, to have a "best friend."

Concepts that can be taught

We can share with parents the information we receive in church school. We can share in the classroom interesting information we get from our parents. Parents are interested in what we learn.

In thinking over things that happened to other people and to ourselves, we can sometimes figure out the reason why they happened. This can help us to understand how God acts in our life. Friendship means receiving and giving: it is a "two-way street."

Contents of curriculum

Our Orthodox past (in terms of family stories). Our parents in our church. Preparing gifts for members of the family on special occasions (Christmas, Mother's and Father's Day, Grandparent's Day). Biblical stories emphasizing the meaning of the family: O.T.: Promise to Abraham of God's blessing to be given to his family; marriage of Isaac (importance of continuing the family); story of Joseph. N.T.: the childhood of Jesus Christ.

Discussion of Bible stories and life situations involving the children's ability to reason out the meaning of the story. O.T. Bible study: Balaam's ass (the man who was afraid to obey God); Jonah (the man who wanted to run away from God); the friendship of David and Jonathan; the friendship of the three youths in Babylon. N.T.: parables like the Prodigal Son (including the older brother); Jesus and Zacchaeus.

Teaching methods

Research carried out by children at home on the history of their family. Some of the parents can give talks to the class on family traditions, on the story of the parish, etc. Studying and making models of all those details of Palestinian life that will help in understanding the New Testament narrative.

Dramatizations, acting out of the stories, helps the children to understand the feeling involved.

3. Community: The role of the school increases and the school world is less protective and less permissive than in the pre-school and first grades. Misunderstandings arise, are experienced and resolved. The opinions and behavior of other children differ from home standards, and the child has to determine where he stands.

How do I act on my own? How do I decide who is right and who is wrong? How can I help others?

Discussion of life situations. N.T. Bible stories: the early Christian community; the first community established after Pentecost; the first deacons; Anania and Saphira; Peter's vision; Paul's conversion.

Assigning simple responsibilities in the classroom. Encouraging two children to work together on a project. Plan class projects for some form of help in the community. The problems and situations of the early Christian community should be described in terms that show their similarity with sitations within the children's experience today.

4. The Church: Mainly perceived as church services. Attitude to attending church services is considerably influenced by the degree of the child's active participation and understanding.

Our church services have a plan, a structure. The things that are done and said in church have a meaning. There are some things that I can do in church.

Study of the Divine Liturgy as a sequence of what the children **see** and **hear** in church. The meaning of what they see. The meaning of their participation: the gifts we bring and the gift we receive in Holy Communion.

Audio-visual aids; making diagrams of the plan of the Divine Liturgy; making posters for its parts: "We hear the Word of God," "What we pray for in the litanies," and so on. (For active participation in the services see Chapter 4 of this book.)

139

Middle childhood: age 8, 9 and 10

Developmental stage

5. World: The child needs to be reassured in his faith in the basic kindliness of the world, to have his trust in life reaffirmed by adults. He is also greatly interested in what he learns at school about the origin of the world, prehistoric creatures etc., and has no idea how it fits with what he is taught of God as creator of all. Religion has to become a unifying way of giving meaning to all knowledge, not a separate subject of instruction.

Concepts that can be taught

There are two ways of knowing what happened: one way is to know **how** it happened, the other way is to know **why** it happened (the meaning of what happened). These are the ways of science and of the Bible respectively. "If God created a good world, why are there so many bad things in it?" "How did evil come into the world?" "Is God stronger than evil?"; children are ready for answers to these questions.

Contents of curriculum

Bible study: story of creation in the light of what the children learn in science in school (this is the time to lay the foundation of an understanding of the relationship between science and religion); the Fall, including explanation of origin of evil; the story of Job; the betrayal of Judas; the Last Supper, Crucifixion and Resurrection of Jesus Christ.

Teaching methods

Textbook material can be supplemented by a number of articles in the children's magazine **Young Life.**

140

6. God: Children try to see God in terms of their rather primitive rationalism, moving away from the realistic fantasy of earlier childhood. His omnipotence and justice, in rather primitive terms, is readily recognized. They tend to accept unquestioningly the existence of God, as well as simple "cause and effect" doctrine, but it is difficult for them to perceive the presence of God in their daily lives. Christ is perceived as a unique person who can work miracles. There is curiosity about the material means of the miracles more than about their meaning.

God acts in our life, in the past and today. God is present in our own life. God the Father, God the Son, and God the Holy Spirit (see explanation suggested on p. 50 of this book).

O.T.: The story of Exodus, with emphasis on how God taught Moses to know Him. N.T.: study of the Twelve Great Feasts and their N.T. readings.

Creative illustration of the stories by the children. Making murals and posters.

141

Middle childhood: age 8, 9 and 10

Developmental stage

7. Prayer and Sacraments: The child's attitude to prayer wavers between formally observing rules imposed by parents and a belief in the magic power of prayer. The more mature children of this age are conscious of certain limitations in what one should pray for. Though most Orthodox children partake of the sacraments of the Eucharist and Confession, the meaning of the sacraments is not clearly understood.

8. Symbolism: Children begin to understand the symbolism of parables and narratives if they deal with actions and feelings within their experience. They are ready to see that a story told about someone can apply to what I feel and what I do.

Concepts that can be taught

What do the prayers we say mean? Learning to understand familiar prayers in terms of their own life experience. What happened when I was baptized? How do we approach Confession? Holy Communion is God's gift to us. Jesus Christ shares His life with us in Holy Communion. What can we bring as our gifts to God?

Concepts like forgiving others, not being boastful, helping those who need help, not judging other people, etc. can be brought home by means of parables.

Contents of curriculum

The Lord's Prayer, study of its meaning in terms of daily life. The meaning of the sacraments of Baptism, Holy Communion and Penance.

Bible: N.T. parables listed under 9 below. Symbolism of the rite of Baptism.

Teaching methods

The purpose of the study of the Lord's Prayer is not its memorization, but making the petitions come alive in examples from the children's experience. Children should be given the opportunity to see the sacrament of Baptism performed.

The Parables adapt themselves very well to dramatization by children. In acting them out, children express their own interpretation of the feelings involved.

142

9. Moralism: Clear-cut moral rules and standards are easily accepted and the authority of parents and teachers is readily recognized. Concept of justice is primitive and harsh. Attitudes are strongly egocentric. Gradually, however, the capacity to recognize one's own fault, to experience repentance and compassion, can become stronger. Evil is still evaluated according to its material gravity and social reprobation.

God wants us to obey Him. He has given us certain laws of how to behave, we try to obey God's laws. The Church has many rules. Children often ask why does the Church have so many rules—meaning rules of external behavior (certain objects in church can be touched by the priest only, rules of fasting, taking off one's hat etc.). They are ready for a concept of disciplined behavior. Its meaning for Christian growth has to be explained.

The story of how Moses received God's law. To present meaningfully the text of the Ten Commandments at this age level is difficult, but the abbreviated form of the Two Great Commandments given in the New Testament (Matt. 22:37; Mark 12:30-33; Luke 10:27) can be explained well. The story of the Sermon on the Mount, quoting those passages that apply to children. Study and discussion of I Cor. 13:4-8.

Everything should be done to convey the importance and impressiveness of God giving a Law. A mural concerning Exodus can involve the work of the whole class. A film might be shown. Models of the stone tables can be made. On the other hand, the discussion of passages from the Sermon on the Mount and of I Cor. 13 should be very simple, taking care that they are at the level of the child's sincere, authentic thinking (i.e. avoid stock verbal formulas that might lead to hypocrisy).

10. Historical consciousness: Better concept of time and space. Greater interest in the truth of the story: "Is it true?". Interest in checking information ("I'll ask my grandfather..."). Budding interest in man's past, especially its physical aspects (cavemen, prehistorical animals). Interest in starting collections. Material details of narrative seem of greater importance than its meaning.

God has a plan for the life of the world. God also acts in the life of individual persons (with major interest in the plot and material details). What did Jesus look like? What was the world like at the time when He lived? How did our church look a long time ago? Were things always like they are now?

Biblical stories and events studied during the year can be presented within the framework Salvation History. The life of Jesus Christ can also be presented as a sequence of events that took place in history and in their proper sequence. The narratives mentioned under **Community** (3) and under **Family** (1) can introduce the child to the concept of a continuing church history.

Making simple charts of the main historical events. Making models illustrating life in Palestine: houses, tents, jars, sheep, shepherds, Tabernacle, etc. Models or illustrations of different type of churches, from the earliest times to the present.

143

Late childhood (pre-adolescence): age 11, 12 and 13

Developmental stage	Concepts that can be taught	Contents of curriculum	Teaching methods
1. Family: Parental influence is less strong than during preceding stage. Nascent criticism of parents prepares for the rebellious period of adolescence. However, there still exists an almost fanatical partisanship of the way things are done at home and a deep need for the moral support given by the home.	What did families contribute to the life of the Church? What is the story of your family? Our parents are not perfect and they, too, ask God to forgive them. They are not always right, but they love us and we love them and obey them. We have responsibilities to the members of our family.	O.T.: the blessing given by God to His people is carried on through family patriarchs; Abraham's willingness to sacrifice his son (human sacrifice changed into concept of "living for God"); Jacob and Esau (Esau's wrong choice of values worse than Jacob's deceit). Lives of saints reflecting family influence (St. Basil the Great) and family conflicts (St. Theodosius of Kiev, St. Sava). Stories of early immigrants and the churches they built.	Discussions on a more mature level involving choices that are not obvious. Bible stories are chosen from this point of view: Jacob "cheats" and "lies," but he has a better understanding of the "hierarchy of values" than Esau has. Abraham's understanding of the sacrifice demanded by God was limited by the concept of human sacrifice prevalent in primitive religions. Lives of saints and stories from modern life help children to understand conflicts in family life. Projects can be carried out that encourage a child's sense of responsibility at home.
2. Self: Growing consciousness of oneself as a person, of one's relationships with others, of happiness and unhappiness, of frustration and achievement. Emotionally	Basic doctrinal ideas can be brought together into a cohesive whole, instead of being presented separately in the form of Bible stories: Salvation History, Redemp-	A summary of one's personal beliefs presented through the study of the Creed. N.T.: problems of personal relationships seen in the study of passages from the	It is important to provide opportunity in class for the children to verbalize and express what they really think: **open-ended stories,** which provide choices of several

144

the child tends to be more settled than during the earlier or later periods. A great amount of factual information is readily accumulated. Concrete generalizations and brief sequences of abstract logic are easily followed. Considerable intellectual confusion in switching from early religious fantasy to a more realistic theology. This confusion expresses itself often in a rather crude sense of humor.

3. **Community:** Influence of school community as a society of peers still very strong, but a process of selection of a smaller, closer group of friends goes on. Girls begin to be interested in boys, but boys prefer to maintain their own group. The world of the teenagers, with their tastes in music, art, clothes etc., seems very attractive to the pre-adolescents and they begin to try to imitate it.

tion, the Kingdom of Heaven, life after death. The meaning of relationships—friendship, responsibility, obedience, loyalty, self-reliance —can be more meaningfully understood in terms of daily life. Learning to make up one's mind and express one's own thoughts and opinions.

Overcoming the "isolation" of religion, the attitude that religion belongs to Sunday and that our daily life in the community of friends and school has nothing to do with it.

Sermon on the Mount, I Cor. 13, I Thess. 5:13-28, and similar ones.

Situations arising within the community (such as racial and ethnic problems, vandalism, gangs, etc.) should be reflected within the curriculum. Any specific situation that involves the children's own reaction can be discussed. Projects can be carried out through which children can be made to realize that there are situations where they can help: visits to lonely old people, invalids. Study of a few lives of early saints who lived in a non-Christian society.

valid solutions to a problem; **role-playing.** Doctrinal truths interpreted in terms of the child's experience of life.

Playing "reporters": having children report on problems or situations with which they have met in daily life, e.g. instances of real courage, and what is involved in it. Discuss the reports in class.

Late childhood (pre-adolescence): age 11, 12 and 13

Developmental stage

4. The Church: Children begin to perceive meanings beyond the external rites, but are still confused about them. More and more they need to involve themselves in action within the church. Need to identify with a few friends or with an adult leader within the church. Conflict between their loyalty to their church and their loyalty to the society of their friends outside the church. They attempt to find rational explanations of the plurality of Christian groups and of religions. More and more they tend to feel that people believe in many different ways and that all ways can be good. The division between the world of the church and of church teachings and the world of everyday concerns grows sharper.

Concepts that can be taught

What difference does it make to me whether I receive Communion or not, whether I am baptized or not? What do sacraments mean? (They are interested in the external rites of the sacraments, but are capable of understanding some of the meaning.) What does it mean when we say "the Church is one" when there are so many churches? How is the Orthodox Church different from other churches and why? Need to feel at home in church through active participation: junior choir, altar boys.

Contents of curriculum

Study of the Sacraments: the rites, the meaning, and some historical background which will help the students to realize how the Church grew. An authoritative text should be provided that explains the problem of the Church's oneness and the plurality of denominations. Introductory concepts of church history.

Teaching methods

As a first step towards dealing with the problem of Christian plurality, we can help children to overcome their parochialism within the Orthodox Church. Visits, followed by discussions, can be arranged to Orthodox churches and institutions of other ethnic backgrounds.

5. The world: Childish concepts are clung to, but doubts and confusions are appearing. The child begins to need to relate and reconcile contradictions. Unless religion is taught in a way to help develop a "one world-view" of life, it will gradually become separated from the rest of life. The critical thinking of the next age level, which often takes place in the context of unbelief and doubts, should be anticipated by encouraging the child to think critically about religion within the context of belief. Evil and conflict are seen as part of human condition.

Science and religion: Do they teach the same thing? Do they contradict each other? Which one is right? Do miracles really happen? How? What about evolution and the Bible story of creation? What happens when people die? These are some of the question the children think about even if they do not ask them in class.

At least one or two lessons should be included each year to deal with the questions and doubts children have at this age. If none can be found in religious educational textbooks, articles from magazines (**Young Life**, for example) and non-Orthodox audio-visual materials can be provided.

The major prerequisite for "science/religion" discussions is the preparedness of the teacher: knowing what science really says and having thought it through in terms of Christian faith.

6. God: Children experience difficulty in adjusting their earlier ideas of God as a kind of glorified Santa Claus to more spiritual concepts. There is danger of their beginning to see "God," "miracles," and "long ago" in contrast to "absence of God," "natural law," and "modern living," with little relation between these two worlds.

Who is God—Father, Son and Holy Spirit? What is Heaven? Do we believe in angels or are they like fairies in fairy-stories? How does God show Himself to me? to me? How do I hear Him? Jesus Christ: why do we call Him "Savior"? "Redeemer"? What does this mean for me?

Concept of the Holy Trinity, taught through the Genesis story of Creation: Creator, Logos (Word) Spirit. O.T. concept of God and how this differed from other religions of those times, cf. Exodus. What Jesus Christ taught us about God: selected passages from the New Testament. Life of St. Gregory Palamas (?).

Children can carry out some simple research in the Bible text with the assistance of the teacher, looking up passages in answer to questions: What did people know about God in the Old Testament? What did Jesus say about God? Children should be encouraged to verbalize their questions and uncertainties.

Late childhood (pre-adolescence): age 11, 12 and 13

Developmental stage

Jesus Christ is perceived rather as a historical person than as a "Savior," with little sense of a personal relation to Him. Theological thought structures, if they are brief and clear, are readily perceived and accepted.

7. **Prayer:** Prayer as an imposed obligation tends to be discarded. "Magic" attitude is still quite strong. Prayers grow less selfish, needs of others are remembered. As children grow more conscious of life's pressures, prayers for protection, for becoming a better person, for forgiveness, become more meaningful and authentic. They are more ready to understand the meaning of sacraments as related to actual needs in daily life.

Concepts that can be taught

Individual prayer now is too private to be talked about in class, but liturgical prayers can be discussed meaningfully. The meaning of major feasts, as expressed in hymns (troparia) and short prayer sequences from sacramental rites, can be made very meaningful.

Contents of curriculum

Study of liturgical prayers: troparia and other prayers connected with special days of the church calendar. Passages from prayers used during the sacraments.

Teaching methods

In an effort to make liturgical texts more meaningful, children can be encouraged to put them in their own words. Children's litanies, hymns and troparia can be made up. Posters illustrating the meaning of psalms and hymns are helpful. Cut-outs from magazines can be used.

148

8. Symbolism: Children are ready now to understand the true symbolism of rites and narratives. There is growing interest in discovering **meanings**, though these meanings must be well within the reach of their comprehension.	Symbols used in the sacraments —bread, wine, water, oil, incense etc.—and their deeper meaning can be understood. Something difficult to understand can be made clearer by a story or an image.	The meaning of symbolic actions and rites in the sacraments. N.T.: the Parables of the Kingdom.	Same as above. Children can be encouraged to "re-tell" parables, in terms of modern life, using objects and actions used today to express the symbolic meaning of the parable.
9. Moralism: Moral sense is still mainly determined by approval or disapproval, but there is a clearer perception of the concept of love in relationships. Though the law of the group is still supreme, a subjectivism begins to develop, which may lead to the rejection of law. There is a tendency to feel dissatisfied with oneself. It is very difficult to establish standards of moral "good taste," given the pressure of standards imposed by our mass media and the desire of the youngsters to imitate older teenagers. Growing capacity for responsibility.	The greatest need is to be able to carry over into the realm of relationships (within the family, within the school community) the concepts of Christian faith. Sin is more than "breaking a rule." Obeying rules is not everything. What wins approval is not always right. A happy ending is not necessarily a material "success story." They can begin to perceive the freedom of choice and the responsibility for the choice that they bear.	Biblical situations involving moral conflict can now be presented. O.T.: Noah's sons, tower of Babel, conflict of Jacob and Esau, Samson, Job, Jonah and others. N.T.: morality, involving repentance and forgiveness; the difference between Peter and Judas; Pontius Pilate; St. Paul. Lives of saints involving conflict and choice (for example St. Vladimir of Kiev).	Moral values are best presented by telling about persons and their actions, then discussing moral rules. It is better to tell a narrative and then have a discussion to resolve the moral issues involved, without oversimplifying the problem. Modern life stories illustrating similar problems are helpful.

Late childhood (pre-adolescence): age 11, 12 and 13

Developmental stage

10. Historical consciousness: Interest in human progress—machines, discoveries, science. Can identify emotionally with the accomplishments of the past. Interest in souvenirs, collections, old photos, museums. Interest in historical sequences, in heroic romantic narratives. Interest in the relationship of history to oneself.

Concepts that can be taught

How did people learn about God in the past? How did our Church become what it is today? How did the Orthodox Church begin in America? How does the Church live in other parts of the world?

Contents of curriculum

Most of the curriculum contents outlined above can now be presented within the framework of historical sequences and historical development. The emphasis, however, should be that we are trying to discover the history of how man learned to know God because it is important for **me today**, that we are not studying history for history's sake.

Teaching methods

Historical charts of events, magazines clippings that illustrate the periods studied, and visits to museums in connection with lessons can all be very helpful.

Adolescence: age 14, 15 and 16

Developmental stage

1. **Family:** The strong emotional desire to be independent and to make their own decisions leads to a resentful and rebellious attitude towards parents and towards adult authority in general. Adolescents want to burst out of the restrictions of childhood, yet they feel insecure when meeting new experiences and new pressures. There is a real conflict between home ties and new social ties outside the home. They need the family as a base of security from which to go out and to which they can return.

Concepts that can be taught

Ideas and principles which adolescents would consider important for **their own future families** provide opportunities for a fresh point of view on family responsibilities and problems.

Contents of curriculum

Study of the sacraments, as an introduction to discussion of the meaning of human life, of human freedom of choice, of good and evil, of our family relationships, of love and hate in family life.

Teaching methods

It is extremely important to keep a balance between **information** and **discussion.** Authentic spontaneous questions by adolescents may come first, and then information must be sought to help find answers. At other times it may be easier to supply information in a thought-provoking way, and this in turn will help to raise questions.

151

Adolescence: age 14, 15 and 16

Developmental stage

2. Self: A new questioning spirit. Increased intellectual ability —formal operational thinking. Increased emotionality. Body changes lead to a disconcerting self-consciousness. Sexual development and new awareness of members of opposite sex. This means ability to reach a level of altruism unknown in childhood, because love becomes a giving as well as a taking. Real tension between the need to be secure and the need to be free. They want to think for themselves but lack sufficient information to do so adequately. Need to be assured of their own worth as individuals.

3. Community: Hunger for significance and status. Need for gradual increase in responsibility. Values powerfully influenced by the

Concepts that can be taught

The questions asked are not "What do we do?" and "What's that?" but **"Why should I?"** and **"How do you know?"**. The two major concepts that absorb them are the discovery of **truth** ("What do I believe?") and **love** ("What does love mean to **me**?"). Authoritarian statements as well their own childish concepts are easily rejected.

Ability to figure out one's own opinion, one's own stand, one's own faith. "I am I," and not merely a member of a group. I have

Contents of curriculum

Religious truth: The Bible: "Why should I believe it?" "What does it mean as a historical document?" "What does it mean as a source of doctrine?" The value of Biblical criticism, the meaning of tradition, historicity of the New Testament as a record of events. The meaning of love: good modern literature can be helpful in focusing on the discovery of self and the meaning of love (e.g. "Love Story"); insights on love from passages in the New Testament.

The history of the early Christian Church (Acts, the Epistles, early martyrs) can serve as an enlightening introduction to the

Teaching methods

The truth of every concept has to be convincingly presented, at the adolescent's own intellectual level. Doubts and questions should be expressed in a permissive atmosphere. The possibility of several answers should be admitted whenever possible.

A research project of what it meant to be a Christian adolescent in the first century and today can be carried out: what it meant at

152

"teenage culture." To dress and behave differently, to express deviating opinions in their adolescent peer group is very difficult. Disapproval by older generation often turns to hostility, returned by the adolescents. Authority of adults must be supported by more than authoritarianism.

4. The Church: The same need for "security in freedom" that is mentioned under **Family** applies here. The Church has to be protective without being repressive. Under the best of circumstances, the Church means to adolescents sympathetic adults whom they love and respect. Occasionally they begin to feel a deeper closeness to God during the church services. The sacrament of Penance becomes more difficult to approach and yet more meaningful. The problem of church pluralism is recognized and causes confusion.

responsibilities within the society in which I live. How do I find them out? Do I want to assume them?

An adolescent's church life either begins to wither, or can become a more personal and real experience. He should be exposed to experiences of worship made meaningful at his level. He can begin to share in some real responsibilities of parish life. They are now ready to understand "What is the Church?" in terms of doctrine.

problems of relationships within a community. Care should be taken to show how we have to face similar situations today.

The meaning of **participation in church life** can be made clearer by exposing adolescents to experiences carried out on their level. The study of church history can provide some understanding of the church situation today. The study of church doctrine should be directed towards the question "What is the Church?"

school, in sports, in the neighborhood, at home, in relationship to social problems (e.g. slavery or racial problems). Illustrated articles, posters, "newspapers," can be worked on.

Teenage retreats, with a complete daily cycle of worship involving their participation. Participation in a junior choir. Choir rehearsals should include brief instruction in the meaning of what is sung and its place in the liturgical structure. Carrying out certain duties during worship services. The study of church history should be presented in units, emphasizing certain basic themes which can be made relevant to the life of the Church today.

Adolescence: age 14, 15 and 16

Developmental stage

5. The World: Adolescents have by now encountered real scepticism, and this leads many to the feeling that religion and science do not mix, that supernatural and natural cannot go together. There is a growth of concern for idealistic causes: freedom, equality, justice.

6. God: God is conceived in more abstract and spiritual terms. Divine communication is thought of rather as internal, subjective in the person receiving it. Yet the less intellectually mature students

Concepts that can be taught

"What do I believe?" is the major question for young people, in the face of the scepticism and the variety of beliefs that they encounter. The actual issues, the questions raised, have to be made clear: What does science say? What do sceptics say? What does materialism teach? Is there a conflict with Christian faith? Where? Why? What can I accept as "my faith"? What is our responsibility in the world as it is today?

Personal faith and knowledge of God is not a matter of classroom instruction. However thoughts about God can be clarified and nurtured by the study of Biblical passages, both O.T. and N.T., about how God

Contents of curriculum

Units on "Faith and Science" should be included in the teaching of doctrine. It is very important that the treatment of "science thinking" and "laws of science" be up-to-date and objective. Much harm can be done by under-estimating the critical ability of this age group. It is very difficult to find a realistic outlet in our church life for the idealistic enthusiasms of young people. So far money-raising seems to be the only activity offered. This raises the whole problem of the missionary work of the Church.

Study of individual lives of saints, with an emphasis on how they acquired knowledge of God: St. Paul, St. Seraphim of Sarov, St. Gregory Palamas. The doctrine of God, as revealed in the Person of

Teaching methods

Money-raising projects can be approached in a more inspiring way, especially if the purpose is one with which the youngsters can identify. It should involve raising money to serve others and not for some convenience for ourselves.

Composing prayers of their own, or re-wording some of the liturgical prayers that are hard to understand.

cling to their childish concepts. Many even stop thinking about religion before they consciously reject it. Content of much religious teaching is felt to be "childish."

7. Prayer: Adolescents are able to recognize the effect of prayer on the one who prays. Personal prayer, no longer imposed by parental discipline, is often given up as a daily habit, but occasional prayers can be sincere and deep.

8. Symbolism: Religious symbolism, whether in liturgical services, in narratives or in doctrine, can be fully understood, especially towards the end of the age period. Rational thought and symbolism can fruitfully complement each other in the presentation of Christian doctrine.

showed Himself. The action of God in the life of individuals can be perceived.

Prayer cannot be "bargaining" with God. Prayer is not "magic." Prayer can be a power in our life. Some people's lives have been deeply affected by prayer.

The symbolic meaning of O.T. narratives can now be readily perceived. The symbolism of sacraments can now be studied not just as external rites, but as images of the meaning of the sacrament.

Jesus Christ, who took upon Himself to suffer for the sins of the world.

Study of short passages on prayer from the writings of the Fathers and of modern Orthodox writers (e.g. the **Diary** of Fr. A. Elchaninoff).

Study of the more difficult parables of the N.T.: the Parables of the Kingdom, the Last Judgment parables. O.T. chapters dealing with Creation and Salvation History.

It is very important to make the young people realize that a "symbolic" meaning does not mean a "fantastic" meaning. What is a "symbolic expression of truth?"

Adolescence: age 14, 15 and 16

Developmental stage	Concepts that can be taught	Contents of curriculum	Teaching methods
9. Moralism: Tendency to discard moral standards determined by approval or disapproval of adults. Interest in discovering one's own standard of right and wrong.	Major emphasis should be on the "Why?" of moral laws. Which rules that belonged to childhood can be discarded? Which ones remain valid? What do I really believe is "good"? What is "bad"?	The more difficult passages of the Sermon on the Mount, which were omitted in the earlier grades, can be presented now and discussed in their application to daily life.	It is important to present history as a continuous process in which we are involved. Problems that had to be solved in the past have to be solved today. It is helpful to take up "themes" of historical development one by one, ending up with their relevance to our time. Making charts, reports, "newspapers" is still helpful.
10. Historical consciousness: Consciousness of living in time, of being carried along by time, is now acquired. Interest in the continuous development of one person or one period. Interest in motives behind past actions.	Most of the concepts mentioned above can be presented in the perspective of their historical development.	Study of church history.	

Select Bibliography

BOWMAN, LOCKE E., *Straight Talk About Teaching in Today's Church,* Philadelphia, Westminster Press [1967]. Excellent and helpful attempt to present church school teaching as "learning how to think along with the pupils."

CULLY, IRIS V., *Ways To Teach Children,* Philadelphia, Fortress Press [1966]. Deals with various aspects of teaching in church school: storytelling, drama, audio-visual aids, music and poetry, research, and various other activities.

CURRAN, DOLORES, *Who, Me Teach My Child Religion?,* Minneapolis, Mine Publications [1970]. A practical and witty approach to a teacher's task.

EMLING, JOHN F., "In the Beginning Was the Response," *Religious Education* Vol. 69 No. 1 (Jan. 1974). A clear, simple presentation of Piaget's theories in their application to religious education.

GODIN, ANDRE, "Some Developmental Tasks in Christian Education," article in the book *Research on Religious Development: A Comprehensive Handbook,* New York, Hawthorne Books, 1971.

GOLDMAN, RONALD, *Readiness for Religion,* New York, Seabury Press [1970]. A basic text for developmental religious education. Part I describes the psychological bases of religious education; part II, the author's concept of the contents and methods of developmental religious education.

GOLDMAN, RONALD, *Religious Thinking from Childhood to Adolescence,* New York, Seabury Press [c. 1964]. Presents the results of a major study of school children's religious ideas. The project was carried out in England, where Bible studies are part of the general school curriculum.

HOLT, JOHN, *How Children Learn* [New York] Dell [c. 1967], and *How Children Fail* [New York, Dell, c. 1964]. A teacher's thoughtful notes and observations on the children's learning processes in a classroom situation. Though the books do not deal with religious education, they are helpful for understanding children's attitudes to the process of learning.

KOHL, HERBERT R., "The Open Classroom," *The New York Review,* 1970.

157

A somewhat dogmatic and negative criticism of public school teaching methods. Some suggestions are helpful in looking for more informal approaches.

KOHLBERG, LAWRENCE, "The Child as a Moral Philosopher," in *Readings in Values Clarification*, ed. Simon and Kischenbaum, Winston Press, 1973. Kohlberg's research resulted in a typological scheme for general structures of moral thought. His research was conducted over a period of twelve years with a group of 75 boys, beginning when they were aged 10-16.

MILLER, RANDOLPH CRUMP, *Education for Christian Living*, Englewood Cliffs, N. J., Prentice-Hall, 1956. Published almost twenty years ago, this book still gives a good and objective approach to the basic task of Christian education in the church. It begins with an outline of the history of Christian education and deals with religious education in the home, in school, in the community and in the church. Methods of teaching and the administration of church school programs are described.

SCHMEMANN, ALEXANDER, *Liturgy and Life: Christian Development Through Liturgical Experience*, Orthodox Church in America, Department of Religious Education, 1974. An indispensable book for all those who are concerned with the Orthodox approach to religious education.